Prayers for the People

Prayers for the People

PEOPLE'S EDITION

Edited by

MICHAEL PERRY

with PATRICK GOODLAND *and* ANGELA GRIFFITHS

MARSHALL PICKERING

An imprint of HarperCollins*Publishers*

JUBILATE   CPAS

Also edited by the Jubilate group:

Hymns for Today's Church
Church Family Worship
Carols for Today
Carol Praise*
Let's Praise!*
Come Rejoice!*
The Wedding Book*
The Dramatised Bible*
Psalms for Today
Songs from the Psalms
Hymns for the People

* Available from HarperCollins

First published in Great Britain in 1992 by Marshall Pickering
Marshall Pickering is an imprint of
HarperCollins*Religious*
Part of HarperCollins*Publishers*
77–85 Fulham Palace Road, London W6 8JB

Designed by Claire Brodmann

Printed in Great Britain by The Bath Press, Avon

A catalogue record for this book is available from the British Library

ISBN 0 551 01990–5 (People's)
ISBN 0 551 01 991–3 (Leader's)

Contents

1 New Year, Thanksgiving for the Old Year   7

2 Epiphany, The Wise Men, The Escape to Egypt   11

3 The People of God, Covenant and Unity   15

4 Following Jesus, Jesus' Teaching   20

5 The Life of Prayer, Forgiveness   25

6 The Family, Parents and Children, Mothering Sunday   28

7 Palm Sunday   33

8 Passiontide, Good Friday, Easter Eve   36

9 Easter, Resurrection   40

10 God's Creation   45

11 Jesus is Lord, Ascension   51

12 The Holy Spirit   55

13 The Holiness and Majesty of God, Trinity   59

14 Sea Theme, Holidays   64

15 God's Love to Us, Our Response   67

16 Invitation to Faith   72

17 The Witnessing Church, The Worldwide Church   76

18 The Caring Church, Healing   82

19 God's Gifts to the Church, Renewal   88

20 The Church: Anniversary, Commitment, Giving   96

21 Harvest Thanksgiving   102

22 Christian Character and Conflict, Our Work, Schools   107

23 Heaven, God's Peace   111

24 Christ's Coming, Judgement   115

25 God's Word to Us, Proclamation   121

26 Christmas   125

27 At a Baptism   130

28 At Holy Communion/The Lord's Supper   132

29 At Local Festivals, For the Peace of the World   147

Acknowledgements   154

A Short Service   156

A Communion Service   158

1.1 GREETING
From Romans 15†

The God of peace be with you all.
Amen.

1.6 RESPONSE
From Revelation 1†

The Lord God says 'I am Alpha and Omega, who is, and who was, and who is to come, the Almighty'. **Amen!**

1.7 RESPONSE
From Psalm 89†

O Lord, we will sing always of your constant love:
**we will proclaim your faithfulness
for ever!**

We know that your love will last for all time:
**that your faithfulness
is founded in heaven.**

Praise be to the Lord for ever:
Amen and Amen!

1.8 RESPONSE
From 2 Corinthians 5†

Anyone in Christ is a new creation:
**the old has gone,
the new has come! Amen.**

1.9 RESPONSE
From Psalm 90†

Lord, you have been our rock in every generation:
**from everlasting to everlasting
you are our God.**

1.12 PRAISE
From Psalm 75†

We give you thanks, O God;
we give you thanks.

We proclaim how great you are,
**and tell of the wonderful things
you have done. Amen.**

1.13 CONFESSION
Diocese of Sheffield, adapted

We look to God for forgiveness, knowing that in the past year we have often grieved him through our failures and sins:

Where we have not cared enough for you:
forgive us, O God.

Where we have not cared enough for your world:
forgive us, O God.

Where we have been content with ourselves as we are:
forgive us, O God.

**Give us the will and the power
to live in the Spirit of Jesus;
now and always. Amen.**

1.14 CONFESSION
Editors

Help us, O Lord, and forgive us when we offer you less than the best of our loyalty and service:

When we resent your loving correction, when we grudge giving to the work of your kingdom, when we fail to value the fellowship of your people; in your tender mercy:
forgive us, Lord, and help us.

When through pride we will not admit our mistakes, when we make it easier for others to do wrong, when we bring upon them anxiety and needless worry; in your tender mercy:
forgive us, Lord, and help us.

For every unkind word we have spoken, for every action which has hurt another

person, for every wrong desire we have
harboured in our minds; in your tender
mercy:
forgive us, Lord, and help us.

**Lord have mercy upon us
and forgive us,
that we may live close to you now
and be with you for ever
in your eternity;
through Jesus Christ our Lord. Amen.**

1.16 COLLECT
Lent 2, ASB 1980

Lord God almighty,
grant your people grace
to withstand the temptations
of the world, the flesh, and the devil,
and with pure hearts and minds
to follow you, the only God;
through Jesus Christ, our Lord. **Amen.**

1.17 PSALM
From Psalm 90†

Lord, you have been our home through
all generations; before the mountains
were born, before you gave birth to the
earth and its people, from everlasting to
everlasting:
you are our God!

A thousand years in your sight are like a
day gone by:
like a dream in the night.

The length of our days is seventy years –
or eighty if we are strong enough:
they quickly pass, and we fly away.

Teach us to count our days:
to gain a heart of wisdom.

Satisfy us every morning with your
unfailing love that we may sing for joy:
and be glad the whole day long.

Make up for our bad days with as many
days of happiness:
**with as many happy years
as our years of sorrow.**

Show us, your servants, your wonderful
deeds:
show your glory to our children.

O Lord our God, let your favour rest
upon us; bless our work and make it
endure:
**yes, Lord,
establish the work of our hands. Amen.**

1.18 PSALM
Psalm 136.1–26†

*The congregation must divide at A, B and C
saying the whole stanza, OR both ministers
and congregation should divide*

> A Give thanks to God, for he is good:
> A **his love shall last for ever!**

> B Give thanks to him, the God of gods:
> B **his love shall last for ever!**

> C Give thanks to him, the Lord of
> lords:
> C **his love shall last for ever!**

> A For God alone works miracles:
> A **his love shall last for ever!**

> B The skies were made at his
> command:
> B **his love shall last for ever!**

> C He spread the seas upon the earth:
> C **his love shall last for ever!**

> A He made the stars to shine at night:
> A **his love shall last for ever!**

> B He made the sun to shine by day:
> B **his love shall last for ever!**

> C He brought us out from slavery:
> C **his love shall last for ever!**

> A He leads us onward by his grace:
> A **his love shall last for ever!**

> B He saves us from our enemies:
> B **his love shall last for ever!**

> C Give thanks to God, for he is good:
> C **his love shall last for ever!**
> ALL **Amen!**

1.19   PSALM
Psalm 147.1–20†

The congregation may divide at A, B and C

O praise the Lord, sing out to God:
such praise is right and good.

The Lord restores Jerusalem:
A **he brings the exiles home.**

He heals all those with broken
hearts:
B **he bandages their wounds.**

He counts the number of the stars:
C **he calls them each by name.**

How great and mighty is the Lord:
A **immeasurably wise!**

He raises up the humble ones:
B **and brings the mighty down.**

Sing hymns of triumph to his name:
C **make music to our God!**

He spreads the clouds across the
sky:
A **he showers the earth with rain.**

He sends the animals their food:
B **he feeds the hungry birds.**

His true delight is not the strong:
C **but those who trust his love.**

· Extol the Lord, Jerusalem:
A **let Zion worship God!**

For God shall keep your people safe:
B **and bring your harvest home.**

He gives commandment to the earth:
C **his will is quickly done.**

He spreads like wool the falling
snow:
A **how cold the frosty air!**

He sends the wind, the warming
rain:
B **and melts the ice away.**

His laws he gives to Israel:
C **and Judah hears his word.**

He does not favour other lands:
ALL **so, praise the Lord. Amen!**

1.21   CREED
From 2 Corinthians 1†

All God's promises are 'yes' in Christ;
through him we give glory to God and
say, 'Amen':

**It is Christ
to whom we belong.**

**It is the Father
who assures us of our salvation
    and anoints us for his service.**

**It is the Spirit
by whom we are sealed in love
    for evermore.**

**We believe in one God:
Father, Son, and Holy Spirit. Amen.**

1.22   FOR THE PRESENCE OF GOD
From Psalms 143†

O God,
as we remember days gone by,
and think about all you have done for us,
our souls thirst for you
and we lift our hands to you in prayer.
Answer us now, O Lord;
don't hide yourself from us,
remind us each morning
of your constant love:
for we put our trust in you,
through Jesus Christ our Lord. **Amen.**

1.25   FOR THE SICK AND THE SAD
Editors

O Lord, as we think of other people hear
our prayer.

For all who are ill (especially . . .), we ask
your healing. Lord in your mercy:
hear our prayer.

For those who are lonely, frightened and
unhappy, we ask your help. Lord, in
your mercy:
hear our prayer.

For those who are suffering from war,
and for refugees, we ask your care. Lord,
in your mercy:
hear our prayer.

For children who are handicapped, we ask your protection. Lord, in your mercy: **hear our prayer.**

For those who are in trouble through foolish behaviour, we ask your correction and restoration. Lord, in your mercy: **hear our prayer.**

For those who are hungry or homeless or in inadequate housing, we ask your compassion. Lord, in your mercy: **hear our prayer.**

For your church in every part of the world, we ask for your compassion. Lord, in your mercy: **hear our prayer.**

For all who labour for the peace of the world and the freedom of all peoples, we ask your guidance and strength. Lord, in your mercy: **hear our prayer.**

Lord, you promise to hear those who are gathered to pray in your name: receive our prayer for all in need, and grant your salvation to them and to us through our Saviour, Jesus Christ. Amen.

1.31   FOR GOD'S HELP
IN THE NEW YEAR
Christopher Idle, adapted

O God our Father, at the beginning of this new year, look upon our Christian family. We come to you in prayer with our hopes and resolutions. And we come also with our doubts and fears, knowing the power of the world, the flesh and the devil. Yet we pray that you will help us not to fall. At the beginning of the new year,
Lord, hear our prayer.

Look upon us as we do our work, face our exams, run our households, look for jobs, earn our wages, maintain our business, enjoy our leisure. At the beginning of the new year,
Lord, hear our prayer.

Look upon our church as it loves and cares and serves, as it learns and worships and witnesses. At the beginning of the new year,
Lord, hear our prayer.

Look upon your world, with all its waste and war and sorrow, yet all its joys as well. At the beginning of the new year,
Lord, hear our prayer.

Father, grant us your presence and your peace; keep us safe in the knowledge of Jesus Christ our Lord. Amen.

1.33   THANKSGIVING
Editors

For the year that is past:
Lord, we thank you.

For your mercies every day:
Lord, we thank you.

For new discoveries of your grace, and fresh opportunities to do your work:
Lord, we thank you.

For your strength to survive hurt and sorrow, and that you pick us up when we fall:
Lord, we thank you.

For our life in Christ which gives us hope for the future:
Lord, we thank you.

Lord, we thank you that you walk beside us – your mighty hand to uphold us, your heart of love to guide us, your outstretched arms to meet us at our journey's end; through Jesus our redeemer. Amen.

1.34   THANKSGIVING (CONCLUSION)
From Ephesians 5†

We give thanks for everything to God the Father:
in the name of our Lord Jesus Christ. Amen.

1.37 ASCRIPTION
From Jude†

Now to him who is able to keep us
    from falling
and to present us
before his glorious presence
without fault and with great joy –
to the only God our Saviour
be glory, majesty,
power and authority,

through Jesus Christ our Lord,
before all ages, now, and for evermore!
Amen.

1.38 DOXOLOGY
Liturgical Commission

In a world of change and hope,
of fear and adventure:
faithful God,
glorify your name. **Amen.**

Epiphany, The Wise Men, The Escape to Egypt.

2.1 GREETING
From 2 John†

Grace, mercy and peace from God the
Father and from Jesus Christ, the
Father's Son, be with you in truth and
love. **Amen.**

2.7 RESPONSE
From Isaiah 60†

Arise, shine, for your light has come:
**the glory of the Lord
has risen upon you. Amen.**

2.8 RESPONSE
From Matthew 2†

We have seen his star in the East:
**and have come with gifts
to worship the Lord. Amen.**

2.9 RESPONSE
From John 1†

We have seen his glory:
**glory as of the only Son
    from the Father. Amen.**

2.11 APPROACH
From John 1, Colossians 1, Hebrews 1†

In the beginning was the Word, and the
Word was with God, and the Word was
God. Through him all things were made.

In him was life and that life was the light
of us all. The light shines in the darkness:
**We have seen his star in the East
and have come to worship him.**

Christ is the image of the invisible God,
the first-born over all creation. He is
before all things, and in him all things
hold together:
**We have seen his star in the East
and have come to worship him**

The Word became flesh and lived for a
while among us. We have seen his glory,
the glory of the one and only Son, who
came from the Father, full of grace and
truth:
**We have seen his star in the East
and have come to worship him.**

In the past God spoke to our forefathers
through the prophets, but in these last
days he has spoken to us by his Son, who
is the radiance of his glory and the exact
representation of his being:
**We have seen his star in the East
and have come to worship him.**

God, who said, 'Let light shine out of
darkness,' made his light shine in our
hearts to give us the light of the
knowledge of the glory of God in the face
of Christ:
**We have seen his star in the East
and have come to worship him. Amen.**

2.12 PRAISE
From Psalm 94†

Come, let us worship the Lord:
let us worship the Lord.

Let us bow down in the presence of our
maker:
he is the Lord our God.

2.13 PRAISE
From Psalm 96†

Sing a new song to the Lord;
sing to the Lord, all the earth!

Sing to the Lord, praise his name;
proclaim his triumph day by day!

Worship the Lord in the splendour of his
holiness;
tremble before him all the earth!

For great is the Lord, and worthy to be
praised.
Amen.

2.14 CONFESSION
Editors

Lord Jesus Christ, wise men from the
East worshipped and adored you; they
brought you gifts – gold, incense, and
myrrh.

We too have seen your glory, but we
have often turned away. Lord, in your
mercy,
forgive us and help us.

We too have gifts, but we have not fully
used them or offered them to you. Lord,
in your mercy,
forgive us and help us.

We too have acclaimed you as King, but
we have not served you with all our
strength. Lord, in your mercy,
forgive us and help us.

We too have acknowledged you as God,
but we have not desired holiness. Lord,
in your mercy,
forgive us and help us.

We too have welcomed you as Saviour,
but we have failed to tell others of your
grace. Lord, in your mercy,
forgive us and help us.

**Make our trust more certain,
make our love more real,
make our worship
    more acceptable to you;
for your glory's sake. Amen.**

2.15 CONFESSION
Editors

Lord Jesus Christ, you continually reveal
your truth to us. Our privilege is the
measure of our responsibility to share
your good news with the world.

When all too easily we receive from you
and neglect to tell others of your coming
to give eternal life: Lord, in your mercy,
forgive us and strengthen us.

When we receive your gracious gifts, and
clutch them to ourselves, and forget to
share them with others: Lord, in your
mercy,
forgive us and strengthen us.

When we know your guidance but trust
in our own desires and selfish opinions:
Lord, in your mercy,
forgive us and strengthen us.

When by our own choice, we walk in
spiritual darkness, and do not recognise
your nearness: Lord, in your mercy,
forgive us and strengthen us.

**Lord, you alone can dispel our darkness:
help us to worship you,
to come into the fullness of your light,
then go out to work for you
    in a darkened world,
for the sake of Jesus Christ our Lord.
Amen.**

2.17 COLLECT
Christmas 2 (year 2), ASB 1980

Eternal God,
who by the shining of a star
led the wise men

to the worship of your Son:
guide by his light
the nations of the earth,
that the whole world
may behold your glory;
through Jesus Christ our Lord **Amen.**

2.18   COLLECT
Holy Innocents, Church of Ireland APB 1984

Heavenly Father,
whose children suffered
at the hands of Herod
though they had done no wrong:
help us to defend all your children
from cruelty and oppression;
in the name of Jesus Christ
who suffered for us,
but is alive and reigns with you
and the Holy Spirit,
one God, now and for ever. **Amen.**

2.19   PSALM
Psalm 95. 1–7†

The congregation may divide at A and B, the ministers at M and N

M Come, let's joyfully praise our God, acclaiming the Rock of our salvation.

N Come before him with thanksgiving, and greet him with melody.

A **Our God is a great God –**
B **a king above all other gods.**
A **The depths of the earth
     are in his hands –**
B **the mountain peaks
     belong to him.**
A **The sea is his – he made it!**
B **His own hands prepared the land.**

M Come, bow down to worship him;
N kneel before the Lord who made us.
A&B **We are his people,
     the sheep of his flock.**

M&N You shall know his power today –
N if you listen to his voice.
     Amen

2.24   CREED
From Titus 2 and 3†

We believe the grace of God has dawned upon us with healing for all the world, and so we rejoice to declare our faith in him:

**We trust in God the Father,
who has revealed his love
and kindness to us,
and in his mercy saved us,
not for any good deed of our own,
but because he is merciful.**

**We trust in Jesus Christ,
who gave himself up for us
to free us from our sin,
and set us apart for himself –
a people eager to do good.**

**We trust in the Holy Spirit,
whom God poured out on us generously
through Christ our saviour,
so that justified by grace
we might become heirs
with the hope of eternal life. Amen.**

2.25   FOR PEOPLE IN NEED
Source unknown, adapted Editors

O God, the Father of our Lord Jesus Christ, you came to bring good news to the poor, sight to the blind, freedom to the oppressed, and salvation to your people. Come to us now by your Holy Spirit and break down the barriers which divide, that we may truly love one another:

Persecuted minorities, all oppressed by sectarian or cold religious attitudes, all oppressed by racist politics and government, all oppressed by force or by intimidation: our God and Father,
these we bring before you.

Those who seek to remove oppression by patience, persuasion, courage and love: our God and Father,
for these we ask your grace.

All who feel compelled to turn to violence to oppose violence – that they

may not be corrupted or oppressive themselves: our God and Father,
for these we pray.

All who are not whole – the hungry, the diseased, the homeless; those in poverty, depression, degradation, all who cannot find community: our God and Father,
for these we shout aloud.

Those who give their lives to bring to others wholeness and salvation: our God and Father,
for these we ask your strength.

Lord Jesus,
make us one in heart and mind,
give us a spirit of service
     and true faith
in Jesus Christ our Lord. Amen.

2.28 LITANY
Editors

Christ, born in a stable,
give courage to all who are homeless;

Christ, who fled into Egypt,
give comfort to all refugees;

Christ, who fasted in the desert,
give relief to all who are hungry;

Christ, who hung in torment on the cross,
give strength to all who suffer;

Christ, who died to save us,
give us the assurance
of your forgiveness;

Save us today,
and use us in your loving purposes;
for your glory's sake. Amen.

2.29 THAT WE MAY HAVE LIGHT
Editors

Lord Jesus, we acknowledge you as the Light of the World:
Lord, lead us from darkness to light.

Lord Jesus, we acknowledge you as the light to the nations:
Lord, help us to reflect

the light of your love.

Lord Jesus, we acknowledge you as the true light from heaven:
Lord, let us always live
in the light of your holiness.

Lord Jesus, we acknowledge you as the light that overcomes the darkness:
Lord, guide us
and shine your light on our daily path.

Lord Jesus, we acknowledge you as the eternal light of our life:
Lord,
we are your children of light,
aglow and ever praising you,
our Sun of Righteousness for ever.
Amen.

2.31 THANKSGIVING
Editors

Eternal God, our loving heavenly Father, you are perfection, yours is the fullness of majesty, power and glory. Yours are the heavens and the earth. Here we bow before you:
and praise you for your greatness.

Through the ages you have concerned yourself with men and women, your creatures on this earth. Within the immensity of this universe our little world has been your delight. Here we bow before you:
and praise you for your greatness.

You have revealed to us glimpses of your eternal glory in your Son our Saviour, Jesus Christ. He is Lord of time and of eternity; he is the living Word who became flesh and lived among us. We have seen his glory, full of grace and truth. Here we bow before you:
and praise you for your greatness.

You, Lord God, have commanded the light to shine out of darkness. You have lit up our minds and our emotions and we are receiving knowledge of you and your gracious dealing through Jesus Christ. Eternal God:
we praise you, adore you,
and bless your holy name;
through Jesus Christ our Lord. Amen.

The People of God, Covenant and Unity

3.1 GREETING
From Galatians 6†

Peace and mercy to the people of God.
Amen.

3.11 RESPONSE
From Psalm 95†

Come, let us bow down in worship, let us
kneel before the Lord our maker:
he is our God;
we are the sheep of his pasture,
the people of his care. Amen.

3.12 RESPONSE
From Psalm 100†

Know that the Lord is God:
It is he who made us, and we are his,
we are his people,
the sheep of his pasture.

3.16 PRAISE
From Psalm 117†

Praise the Lord, all you nations;
extol him, all you peoples!

For his love protecting us is strong;
his faithfulness endures for ever! Amen.

3.17 PRAISE
From Psalm 72†

Praise the Lord, the God of Israel:
he alone does marvellous things.

Praise his glorious name for ever;
let his glory fill the earth!
Amen. Amen.

3.18 PRAISE
From Revelation 19†

Praise our God, all you his servants, you
who fear him both small and great:
Alleluia!

Alleluia!
Salvation and glory and power
belong to our God,
true and just are his judgements.
Alleluia! Amen!

3.19 CONFESSION
Editors

Father God, we thank you for calling us
and making us your children:

In bringing us out of spiritual darkness
and giving us light, you desire that we
should be clearly seen as your people.
When we fail to live up to your
expectations – Father, be merciful:
forgive us and help us.

When we show uncaring attitudes; when
our selfish desires are revealed in our
life-style – Father, be merciful:
forgive us and help us.

When we become mesmerised by trivial
things of this world, and forget
important things which belong to your
kingdom – Father, be merciful:
forgive us and help us.

When we hold on to petty differences in
the practice of our faith, and fail to show
the unity of your family – Father, be
merciful:
forgive us and help us.

Father, purify us continually;
make us die to self
and rise to newness of life
in Jesus Christ our Lord. Amen.

3.20 CONFESSION
From Daniel 9†

O Lord our God, you brought your
people out of slavery with a mighty
hand, and made for yourself a name
which endures to this day:

→

We have sinned, we have done wrong.
O Lord, hear:
O Lord, forgive!

In keeping with all your righteous acts,
turn away your anger from your people.
O Lord, hear:
O Lord, forgive!

Our sins have made us despised by those
around us. O Lord, hear:
O Lord, forgive!

We do not come before you because we
are righteous, but because of your great
mercy. O Lord, hear:
O Lord, forgive!

**O Lord our God, do not delay
but send your holy Spirit
to revive your church,
because your people
bear the name of Christ. Amen.**

3.21 CONFESSION
From Isaiah 59†

**O God,
our offences are many in your sight,
and our sins testify against us;
our wrongdoing is ever with us,
and we acknowledge our iniquities;
we have rebelled against you
and acted treacherously towards you
turning our backs on you:
O God, forgive us,
through Jesus Christ our Lord. Amen.**

3.23 COLLECT
Sixth Sunday before Christmas, ASB 1980

Lord God our redeemer,
you heard the cry of your people
and sent your servant Moses
  to lead them out of slavery:
free us from the tyranny of sin and death
and, by the leading of your Spirit,
bring us to our promised land;
through Jesus Christ our Lord. **Amen.**

3.24 COLLECT
Seventh Sunday before Easter, ASB 1980

Merciful Lord,
grant to your faithful people
pardon and peace:
that we may be cleansed from all our sins
and serve you with a quiet mind;
through Jesus Christ our Lord. **Amen.**

3.25 COLLECT
Pentecost 2, Church of Ireland APB 1984

Almighty and eternal God,
you have called us to be your people:
bring us to closer unity and fellowship
with you and one another,
so that every member of your Church
may serve you in holiness and truth;
through our Lord and Saviour
  Jesus Christ. **Amen.**

3.26 PSALM
Psalm 105.1–45†

*The congregation – and ministers/leaders –
may divide at A, B and C*

Give thanks to the Lord, praise his
name:
A **tell the nations what he has done.**

Sing to him, sing praise to him:
B **tell of all his wonderful deeds.**

Glory in his holy name:
C **let all who worship him rejoice.**

Go to the Lord for help:
A **and worship him for ever.**

Remember the wonders he does:
B **the miracles he performs.**

He is the Lord our God:
C **he judges the whole wide earth.**

He keeps his word and covenant:
A **for a thousand generations.**

The covenant he made with
Abraham:
B **the oath he swore to Israel.**

He brought them out of Egypt:
c **and none of them was lost.**

He gave a cloud for covering:
A **a pillar of fire by night.**

He gave them bread from heaven:
B **and water from the rock.**

He brought his people out rejoicing:
c **his chosen ones with shouts of joy.**
ALL **Praise the Lord! Amen**

3.28 CREED
From 1 Corinthians 8 and 12†

There is one God and Father:
from him all things come.

There is one Lord Jesus Christ:
through him we come to God.

There is one Holy Spirit:
in him we are baptised into one body.

**We believe and trust in one God:
Father, Son and Holy Spirit. Amen.**

3.29 CREED
From Ephesians 4†

As God's people, let us declare our faith:

**There is one body and one Spirit,
just as we were called to one hope;
one Lord, one faith, one baptism:
one God and Father of all,
who is over all, and through all,
and in all. Amen.**

3.33 FOR UNITY IN THE SPIRIT
From Romans 1†

God our Father,
always when we pray
we thank you for our fellowship
with others whom you love
and whom you have called
    to be your own people:
help us to share with them
our spiritual blessings,
and so to be made strong together –
our faith helping them
and their faith helping ours;
through Jesus Christ our Lord. **Amen.**

3.35 FOR GOD'S GRACE
Editors

O God, we are your people: in your Son
you have redeemed us; by your Spirit
you have sealed us as your own.

Make our hearts respond to your love.
Lord, receive our praise,
and hear our prayer.

Make our lives bear witness to your
mercy. Lord, receive our praise,
and hear our prayer.

Make our wills ready to obey. Lord,
receive our praise,
and hear our prayer.

**Show us your glory,
that we may delight in your presence,
and walk with you faithfully
all our days. Amen.**

3.38 FOR FORGIVENESS
From Exodus 34†

Lord, the only God,
compassionate and gracious,
slow to anger, full of love:
be with us now.
Judge of the guilty:
though we have been stubborn,
though we have rebelled against you,
yet forgive our wickedness and sin
and receive us as your own;
through Jesus Christ our Lord. **Amen.**

3.40 THANKSGIVING
From 1 Corinthians 12†

We thank God for our unity in diversity.

There are different kinds of gifts:
but the same Spirit.

There are different kinds of service:
but the same Lord.

There are different kinds of working:
but the same God.

**Praise to God almighty,
Father, Son and Holy Spirit,
who works in us
in all these ways. Amen.**

3.43 DEDICATION (UNITY)
Unknown

God our Father,
in the name of Christ
and in the power of the Spirit,
we commit ourselves
to you and to one another,
to live, work and pray
as one body in Christ;
to do apart
nothing which we can do together,
and to do together
what we cannot do apart.
Give us vision,
give us courage,
and give us joy,
that the world may believe
that Jesus is Lord
to your eternal glory. Amen.

3.44 THE TEN COMMANDMENTS
From Exodus 20/Deuteronomy 5†

Let us hear the decrees and the laws of
the Lord, learn them, and be sure to
follow them:

'You shall have no other gods but me':
Lord, help us to love you
with all our heart, all our soul,
all our mind and all our strength.

'You shall not make for yourself any
idol':
Lord, help us to worship you
in spirit and in truth.

'You shall not dishonour the name of the
Lord your God':
Lord, help us to honour you
with reverence and awe.

'Remember the Lord's day and keep it
holy':
Lord, help us to celebrate Christ
risen from the dead,
and to set our minds on things above,
not on things on the earth.

'Honour your father and your mother':
Lord, help us to live as your servants,
giving respect to all,
and love to our brothers and sisters
in Christ.

'You shall not murder':
Lord, help us to be reconciled
with each other,
and to overcome evil with good.

'You shall not commit adultery':
Lord, help us to realise
that our body
is a temple of the Holy Spirit.

'You shall not steal':
Lord, help us to be honest in all we do,
and to care for those in need.

'You shall not be a false witness':
Lord, help us always to speak the truth.

'You shall not covet anything which
belongs to your neighbour':
Lord, help us to remember Jesus said,
'It is more blessed to give
than to receive',
and help us to love our neighbours
as ourselves;
for his sake. Amen.

3.45 DEDICATION
From Deuteronomy 26†

Choose for yourselves this day whom
you will serve:
We will serve the Lord!

You are witnesses against yourselves that
you have chosen to serve the Lord:
Yes, we are witnesses.

Serve no other gods; yield your hearts to
the Lord your God:
We will serve the Lord our God
and obey him. Amen.

3.46 ACT OF COMMITMENT (THE
TEN COMMANDMENTS)
From Exodus 20/Deuteronomy 5†

Let us resolve to follow the decrees and
the laws of the Lord:

Lord, we will have no other God
but you.

Lord, we will not make idols
for ourselves,
nor will we worship them.

Lord, we will not dishonour your name.

Lord, we will remember your day
and keep it holy.

Lord, we will honour
our father and our mother.

Lord, we will do no murder.

Lord, we will not commit adultery.

Lord, we will not steal.

Lord, we will not be a false witness.

Lord, we will not covet anything
that belongs to another.

May the awe of your presence
and the vision of your glory
keep us from sinning,
for the sake of Jesus our redeemer.
Amen

3.48 ASCRIPTION
From Revelation 5†

You are worthy, O Lord our God:
to receive glory and honour and power.

For you created all things:
and by your will they existed
and were created.

Your are worthy, O Christ, for you were slain:
and by your blood
you ransomed us for God.

From every tribe and tongue and people and nation:
you made us a kingdom of priests
to serve our God.

To him who sits upon the throne, and to the Lamb
be blessing and honour
and glory and might
for ever and ever. Amen.

3.49 ASCRIPTION (BEFORE SONG)
From Exodus 5†

Who is like you, O Lord, our God –
majestic in holines, awesome in glory,
working wonders?

In your unfailing love you will lead your redeemed;
in your strength
you will guide us, Lord.

Let us sing to the Lord for he is highly exalted:
the Lord will reign
for ever and ever. Amen.

3.50 NIGHT PRAYER
Jim Cotter

O God of love and mercy,
grant us tonight,
with all your people,
rest and peace. **Amen.**

3.51 BLESSING
From 1 Kings 8†

Praise to the Lord, who has given rest to his people:
not one word of all his promises
has failed.

May the Lord your God be with *you:*
may he never leave us
or forsake us.

May he turn *your* hearts to him, to walk in his ways and to keep his commandments:
may the words we have prayed
before the Lord our God
be near him day and night.

Let all the people of the earth know the Lord is God:
there is no other! Amen.

3.57 BLESSING
From Psalm 128†

The Lord bless *you* all the days of *your* life; may *your* community prosper; may *your* families flourish:
peace be upon the Lord's people.

The blessing of God the Father, God the Son and God the Holy Spirit be with *you* always. **Amen.**

Following Jesus, Jesus' Teaching

4.1 GREETING
From Ephesians 6†

Grace to all who love our Lord Jesus Christ with an undying love. **Amen.**

4.8 RESPONSE
From John 6†

Lord, to whom shall we go?
you have the words of eternal life.

4.9 RESPONSE
From 2 Timothy 1†

God did not give us a spirit of timidity:
**but of power, of love
and of self-discipline. Amen.**

4.10 RESPONSE
From Hebrews 12†

Let us fix our eyes on Jesus:
the author and goal of our faith. Amen.

4.11 APPROACH
From 'New Every Morning'

Heavenly Father, from our hearts we thank you for the light of this new day. May we so spend its hours in the perfect freedom of your service, that when evening comes we may again give you thanks. Direct and control us in every part of our life:

Our tongues, that we speak no false or angry words –
Lord, keep us from wrong-speaking

Our actions, that we may do nothing to shame ourselves or hurt others –
Lord, keep us from wrong-doing

Our minds, that we may think no evil or bitter thoughts –
Lord, keep us from wrong-thinking

Our hearts, that they may be set only on pleasing you –
**Lord, keep us in your love,
through Jesus Christ our Lord. Amen.**

4.12 PRAISE
From Psalm 113†

Praise the Lord, you servants of the Lord;
praise the name of the Lord.

Blessed be the name of the Lord;
both now and evermore. Amen.

4.13 CONFESSION
Editors

Almighty God, our Father, we come to you with humble hearts, to confess our sins:

For turning away from you, and ignoring your will for our lives: Father, forgive us,
save us and help us.

For behaving just as we wish, without thinking of you: Father, forgive us,
save us and help us.

For failing you – not only by what we do, but also by our thoughts and words: Father, forgive us,
save us and help us.

For letting ourselves be drawn away from you by temptations in the world about us: Father, forgive us,
save us and help us.

For acting as if we were ashamed to belong to your dear Son Jesus: Father, forgive us,
save us and help us.

Father, we have failed you often, and humbly ask your forgiveness:
**help us so to live
that others may see your glory;
through Jesus Christ our Lord. Amen.**

4.14   CONFESSION
From Psalm 101†

**Lord God, our hearts are guilty,
we have been dishonest,
we have looked on evil,
we have clung to our selfish ways.
We have talked about others
      behind their backs
with haughty eyes and a proud heart.
Lord, forgive us and help us;
renew us in righteousness
      every morning:
make our lives faithful
and our talk blameless
that we may live in your presence
      for ever;
through Jesus Christ our Lord. Amen.**

4.15   A PERSONAL CONFESSION
Editors

**Jesus, my strength, my love, my life,
I have sinned against you
and I now humbly confess it.
I am sorry, Jesus.
Please forgive me
and restore me to spiritual health:
for in you I find my rest,
      my peace, my joy –
in you I am complete. Amen.**

4.17   COLLECT
9 before Easter ASB 1980

Eternal God,
whose Son Jesus Christ is for all people
the way, the truth and the life:
grant us to walk in his way,
to rejoice in his truth,
and to share his risen life;
who is alive and reigns with you
and the Holy Spirit,
one God, now and for ever. **Amen.**

4.18   COLLECT
Pentecost 18, ASB 1980

Almighty God,
you have made us for yourself,
and our hearts are restless
till they find their rest in you:

teach us to offer ourselves
      to your service,
that here we may have your peace,
and in the world to come
      may see you face to face;
through Jesus Christ our Lord. **Amen.**

4.19   PSALM
Psalm 40.4–16†

*The congregation – and ministers – may
divide at A and B.*

Happy are those who trust in God:
who do not worship idols.

Sacrifice and offering you do not
desire:
A **but you want my ears to be open.**

So I said, 'Lord I come:
B **obedient to your word.'**

I delight to do your will, O God:
A **and keep your teaching in my heart.**

I'll tell the world your saving news:
B **you know my lips
will not be sealed.**

I have not hid your righteousness:
A **but speak of all your salvation,
Lord.**

I do not hide your faithful love:
B **but share your mercy with them all.**

May all who come to you be glad;
may all who know your saving
power for ever say:
ALL **How great is the Lord! Amen.**

4.21   READING: THE BEATITUDES
Matthew 5.3–12

Happy are those who know they are
spiritually poor:
**The Kingdom of heaven
belongs to them!**

Happy are those who mourn:
God will comfort them!

Happy are those who are humble:
**They will receive
what God has promised!**

→

Happy are those whose greatest desire is to do what God requires:
God will satisfy them fully!

Happy are those who are merciful to others:
God will be merciful to them!

Happy are the pure in heart:
They will see God!

Happy are those who work for peace:
God will call them his children!

Happy are those who are persecuted because they do what God requires:
**The Kingdom of heaven
    belongs to them!**

Happy are you when people insult you and persecute you and tell all kinds of evil lies against you because you are Christ's disciples. Be happy and glad, for a great reward is kept for you in heaven.

[This is] the word of the Lord.
Thanks be to God.

OR

This is the Gospel of Christ/This is the Gospel of the Lord.
Praise to Christ our Lord/Praise to you, Lord Jesus Christ.

4.22   CREED
From 1 Corinthians 8 and 12†

There is one God and Father:
from him all things come.

There is one Lord Jesus Christ:
through him we come to God.

There is one Holy Spirit:
in him we are baptized into one body.

**We believe and trust in one God:
Father, Son, and Holy Spirit. Amen.**

**4.23   FOR STRENGTH
        TO FOLLOW JESUS**
Unknown

Jesus said: 'If one of you wants to be great, he must be the servant of the rest' – Master, we hear your call:
help us to follow.

Jesus said: 'Unless you change and become humble like little children, you can never enter the Kingdom of heaven' – Master, we hear your call:
help us to follow.

Jesus said: 'Happy are those who are humble; they will receive what God has promised' – Master, we hear your call:
help us to follow.

Jesus said: 'Be merciful just as your Father is merciful; love your enemies and do good to them' – Master, we hear your call:
help us to follow.

Jesus said: 'Love one another, just as I love you; the greatest love a person can have for his friends is to give his life for them' – Master, we hear your call:
help us to follow.

Jesus said: 'Go to all peoples everywhere and make them my disciples, and I will be with you always, to the end of the world' – Master, we hear your call:
help us to follow.

**Lord, you have redeemed us
and called us to your service:
give us grace to hear your word
and to obey your command;
for your mercy's sake. Amen.**

4.24   ABOUT OUR DISCIPLESHIP
From 'New Every Morning'

Lord Jesus, you have called us to the life of discipleship: make us better disciples. You have taught us something of your truth: teach us still more. O Lord, hear us:
Lord, hear us and help us.

Give us at all times openness of mind and humility of heart, that we may learn your will and follow you more closely. O Lord, hear us:
Lord, hear us and help us.

As you have called us to be your disciples, so make us ready to learn all that you wish to teach us. O Lord, hear us:
Lord, hear us and help us.

Open our eyes to your truth,
open our ears to your call;
and in the tasks of life
strengthen us to seek your will
and serve your kingdom. Amen.

4.25 FOR STRENGTH TO OBEY JESUS
From Matthew 22 and John 13†

We pray for God's strength to keep Jesus'
commandments:

'Love the Lord your God with all your
heart, with all your mind, with all your
soul, and with all your strength':
Lord, help us to obey.

'Love your neighbour as yourself':
Lord, help us to obey.

'Love one another as I have loved you':
Lord, help us to obey.

**In your mercy strengthen us
and move our hearts to do your will.
Amen.**

4.28 FOR OUR DAILY LIVES
Editors

Lord God our Father, grant us to know
your control throughout this day. Give
us grace that we may live each hour
conscious of your presence.

Guard our tongues from careless and
unhelpful words, from all false and
uncontrolled speaking; Lord, have mercy
on us:
guard us today.

Fill our minds with your truth, that we
may think no bitter, unkind or evil
thoughts; Lord, have mercy on us:
fill us today.

Save us from actions which hurt and
bring discredit upon ourselves, our
families and you, our God; Lord, have
mercy on us:
save us today.

Let your word of truth live in us richly,
and let the mind of Jesus captivate our
minds:
enable us to please you

and bring honour to your name
through Jesus Christ our Saviour.
Amen.

4.32 TO BE DISCIPLES
Editors

Lord Jesus, when Peter, James and John
heard your voice, they left their nets to
follow you. We want to be followers too:
**teach us your ways,
show us the right path
and, if we are slow to obey,
draw closer and call us again, Lord.
Amen.**

4.33 FOR OUR DAILY WALK
WITH CHRIST
Editors

Lord Jesus,
help us to be aware of your presence
    each day
so that we do not squander
a single moment of our lives;
keep us eager to hear your voice
so that we are ready to obey you
    when you call.
Jesus, please make us a blessing
    in the world,
and let us follow
in the steps of our beloved Master,
to whom be all glory for ever. **Amen.**

4.34 FOR FAITH IN GOD'S LEADING
From 'A New Zealand Prayer Book'

Holy and eternal God,
give us such trust in your sure purpose,
that we measure our lives
not by what we have done or failed to do,
but by our faithfulness to you;
in Jesus our Redeemer. **Amen.**

4.36 COMING TO CHRIST:
A PERSONAL PRAYER
Editors

Lord, in your love and mercy you are still
calling sinners to repentance, calling
stray sheep to the fold, calling prodigal

sons to come home, calling all who
labour and are heavy laden, calling new
disciples to follow you:
Lord of Glory,
in your love and mercy say the word –
and I will come. Amen.

4.37 FOR OUR DAILY WALK
WITH CHRIST
Attributed to Richard of Chichester

Lord Jesus Christ,
redeemer, friend and brother:
may we know you more clearly,
love you more dearly,
and follow you more nearly,
day by day. **Amen.**

4.39 THANKSGIVING FOR
JESUS' PRESENCE
Editors

Lord Jesus,
thank you for being our friend:
when we are weak, you strengthen us,
when we are lonely you speak to us,
when we are sad you comfort us,
when we are glad you rejoice with us;
you are our guide and keeper,
our shepherd and shield;
your presence is our constant joy. **Amen.**

4.40 THANKSGIVING
Editors

For the wonder of creation, we give you
thanks, O Lord:
and praise your holy name.

For Christ, your Living Word, through
whom we are taught the perfect way of
life, we give you thanks, O Lord:
and praise your holy name.

For the gifts and talents with which each
of us is endowed, we give you thanks, O
Lord:
and praise your holy name.

For the blessing of home and family life,
for companionship and true friendship,
we give you thanks, O Lord:
and praise your holy name.

Glory to the Father and to the Son
and to the Holy Spirit
as it was in the beginning
is now, and shall be for ever. Amen.

4.41 FOR OBEDIENCE
From 'The Promise of His Glory'

Lord Jesus Christ,
Son of the Living God:
teach us to walk in your way
    more trustfully,
accept your truth more faithfully,
and share your life more lovingly;
so that we may come
by the power of the Holy Spirit
as one family
to the kingdom of the Father
where you live for ever and ever. **Amen.**

4.42 DEDICATION
Editors

Father,
we dedicate ourselves
to serve you faithfully
and to follow Christ,
to face the future with him,
seeking his special purpose for our lives.
Send us out to work and to witness
    freely, gratefully and hopefully,
in the power of the Spirit,
and for the honour and glory
    of your Son,
Jesus our Lord. **Amen.**

4.43 DEDICATION
From Deuteronomy 10†

O Lord our God,
we want to fear you,
to walk in your ways,
to love and serve you with all our heart
    and all our soul,
and to obey your commandments;
for you are God of gods
    and Lord of lords,
the great one, mighty and awesome:
you are our God,
and we praise you for ever. **Amen.**

The Life of Prayer, Forgiveness

5.1 GREETING

From 2 Timothy 4†

The Lord be with your spirit:
grace be with you. Amen.

5.7 RESPONSE
From Hebrews 10†

We have a great High Priest over the house of God:
**let us draw near to God
with a sincere heart
in full assurance of faith. Amen.**

5.8 RESPONSE
From Ephesians 6†

Pray in the Spirit on all occasions with all kinds of prayers and requests:
be alert and always keep on praying.

5.9 RESPONSE
From Psalm 51†

The sacrifice of God is a broken spirit:
**a broken and contrite heart, O God
you will not despise.**

5.10 RESPONSE
From Daniel 9†

The Lord our God is merciful and forgiving:
**even though we have rebelled
   against him.**

5.11 RESPONSE
From Lamentations 3†

The Lord's compassions never fail; they are new every morning:
Great is your faithfulness, O Lord.

The Lord is good to those whose hope is in him; to the one who seeks him:
**It is good to wait quietly
for the salvation of the Lord.**

5.12 RESPONSE
From 1 Corinthians 15†

The sting of death is sin, and the power of sin is the law:
**But thanks be to God:
he gives us the victory
through our Lord Jesus Christ. Amen.**

5.15 PRAISE
From Psalm 80†

Turn to us, almighty God;
look down from heaven and see!

Renew us, O Lord God almighty;
**show us your mercy
that we may be saved!**

5.16 CONFESSION
Editors

Gracious God, we confess our shortcomings and our sins. How slow we are to do good! In your mercy:
Lord, forgive us.

How easily we are deceived by passing values of the world! In your mercy:
Lord, forgive us.

How weak is our hold on things which are eternal! In your mercy:
Lord, forgive us.

How glibly we blame and criticise others, and how slow we are to blame ourselves! In your mercy:
Lord, forgive us.

**Give us your pardon,
give us liberty;
help us not to be slaves
   to insecurity, doubt, and guilt;
help us to claim your promises
as we confess our sins;
through Jesus our Lord. Amen.**

5.17 CONFESSION
From Psalm 51†

The sacrifices of God are a broken spirit;
a broken and contrite heart, O God, you
will not despise. O God, in your unfailing
love:
have mercy on us.

We know our transgressions, and our sin
is ever before us; against you only have
we sinned and done what is evil in your
sight. O God, in your unfailing love:
have mercy on us.

According to your great compassion blot
out our transgressions, wash away all
our iniquity and cleanse us from our sin.
O God, in your unfailing love:
have mercy on us.

**Cleanse us, and we shall be clean;
wash us,
 and we shall be whiter than snow;
through Jesus Christ our Lord. Amen.**

5.21 COLLECT
Pentecost 22, Church of Ireland APB 1984

Almighty God,
you gave your Son Jesus Christ
to break the power of evil:
free us from all darkness and temptation,
and bring us to eternal light and joy;
through the power of him
who lives and reigns
with you and the Holy Spirit,
one God, now and ever. **Amen.**

5.22 COLLECT
From Concluding Prayers, ASB 1980

Almighty God,
the fountain of all wisdom,
you know our needs before we ask,
and our ignorance in asking:
have compassion on our weakness,
and give us those things
which for our unworthiness we dare not,
and for our blindness we cannot ask,
for the sake of your Son,
Jesus Christ our Lord. **Amen.**

5.23 PSALM
Psalm 80.1–19†

Ministers/leaders may divide at A, B and C

A Hear us, O Shepherd of Israel, leader
   of your flock.

B Hear us from your throne above the
   cherubim.

C Shine forth, awaken your strength,
   and come to save us.
   **Bring us back, O God, and save us,
   make your face to shine upon us.**

A O Lord God almighty, how long will
   you be angry with your people's
   prayers?

B You have given us sorrow to eat and
   tears to drink.

C You have made us a source of
   contention to our neighbours, and our
   enemies insult us.
   **Bring us back, O God, and save us,
   make your face to shine upon us.**

A Return to us, O God Almighty, look
   down from heaven and see.

B Look on this vine that you planted
   with your own hand, this child you
   raised for yourself.

C Let your hand rest upon the people
   you have chosen, then we will not
   turn away from you; revive us, and
   we shall praise your name.
   **Bring us back, O God, and save us,
   make your face to shine upon us.
   Amen.**

5.25 CREED
From Hebrews 4†

Let us hold firmly to the faith we profess:

**We have a high priest
able to understand our weaknesses
who has gone into heaven:
Jesus, the Son of God.
He was tempted in every way,
just as we are – yet without sin.**

**Therefore we approach
the throne of grace
with confidence,
to receive mercy
and find grace to help us
in our time of need. Amen.**

5.27 AFTER PRAYER
From the Lima Liturgy

Into your hands, O Lord,
we commend all for whom we pray,
trusting in your mercy;
through your Son, Jesus Christ, our Lord.
Amen.

5.29 FOR FRANKNESS BEFORE GOD
From 'A New Zealand Prayer Book'

All-seeing God,
teach us to be open with you
    about our needs,
to seek your support in our trials,
to admit before you our sins,
and to thank you for all your goodness;
for Jesus' sake. **Amen.**

5.30 FOR FORGIVENESS
From 'A New Zealand Prayer Book'

God of infinite love,
grant that we who know your mercy
may rejoice in your forgiveness
and gladly forgive others;
for the sake of Jesus Christ our Saviour.
Amen.

5.36 THAT WE MAY LIVE IN GOD
From Philippians 4†

O God of peace,
cause us to rejoice in you always,
make us gentle to everyone;
keep us from being anxious
    about anything –
help us to ask you for what we need,
    with thanksgiving;
and let your peace
guard our hearts and minds
in Jesus Christ our Lord. **Amen.**

5.39 LITANY
From 'Contemporary Parish Prayers'

By the prayers of Jesus,
Lord, teach us how to pray.

By the grace of Jesus,
Lord, teach us how to give.

By the labours of Jesus,
Lord, teach us how to work.

By the love of Jesus,
Lord, teach us how to love.

By the cross of Jesus,
Lord, teach us how to live. Amen.

5.40 A MORNING PRAYER
From Isaiah 33†

O Lord,
be gracious to us –
we long for you.
Be our strength every morning,
our salvation in time of distress.
Thank you, Lord. **Amen.**

5.42 AN EVENING PRAYER
Frank Colquhoun

O God of all life,
thank you for looking after us today
and for all your goodness to us:
bless us tonight with your forgiveness,
send your peace into our hearts,
and take us and all we love
    into your care;
for Jesus Christ our Saviour's sake. **Amen.**

5.45 THANKSGIVING
From Psalm 118†

God our Father, we thank you,
for you are good,
and your love endures for ever;
we thank you that you have heard
    our cry to you
and set us free;
we thank you that you are with us,
and we need not be afraid;
we thank you that you have answered us
and become our salvation;
through Jesus our Lord. **Amen.**

5.46   ASCRIPTION
From Jude†

Now to him who is able to keep us
   from falling,
and to present us faultless
before the presence of his glory,
with exceeding joy;
to the only wise God, our Saviour,
be glory and majesty,
   dominion and power,
both now and for ever. **Amen.**

5.52   CONCLUDING PRAISE
From Exodus 33†

Lord God almighty, you have revealed
your goodness to us and proclaimed
your name among us:
show us your glory.

You will have mercy on us, and
compassion; in Christ you will forgive
our sins:
**hide us in the cleft of the Rock,
cover us with your hand.**

Lord, you know us by name; in Christ we
have found favour in your sight:
**now let your presence go with us,
and give us rest. Amen.**

The Family, Parents and Children, Mothering Sunday

6.1   GREETING
From 3 John†

Peace to you . . . greet your friends by
name. **Amen.** *(We greet each other)*

6.8   RESPONSE
From Ephesians 3†

I bow my knees before the Father:
**from whom every family in
heaven and on earth is named.**

6.9   RESPONSE
From Psalm 16†

We have set the Lord always before us:
**because he is at our right hand,
we will not be shaken.**

6.11   APPROACH
From Deuteronomy 12†

Lord, our God,
this is the place
   where we may worship you;
you have set your name here.
Here in your presence
our families shall rejoice,

because you have blessed us;
here we present to you
the offering of our lives;
here we promise
   to obey your laws;
here we pray for our children,
that we and they
may do what is right in your sight;
through Jesus our Redeemer. **Amen.**

6.13   PRAISE
From Psalm 95†

Come, let us sing for joy to the Lord;
let us shout to the Rock of our salvation.

Come before him with thanksgiving;
sing him joyful songs of praise! Amen.

6.14   CONFESSION
From Ephesians 5 and 6, Editors†

*The the bracketed section may be omitted

O God, the Father of us all, we come to
you in sorrow, for we have often failed
you:
Lord, forgive us, and help us to obey.

You have taught us: 'Honour your father and mother, that it may go well with you and that you may enjoy long life on the earth.' We have often failed you:
Lord, forgive us, and help us to obey.

You have taught us as children: 'Obey your parents in the Lord, for this is right.' We have often failed you:
Lord, forgive us, and help us to obey.

You have taught us as fathers: 'Do not exasperate your children; instead, bring them up in the training and instruction of the Lord.' We have often failed you:
Lord, forgive us, and help us to obey.

You have taught us as mothers to live with sincere faith and bring our children to Christ. We have often failed you:
Lord, forgive us, and help us to obey.

*[You have taught us as husbands: 'Love your wives as you love yourselves.' We have often failed you:
Lord, forgive us, and help us to obey.

You have taught us as wives: 'Respect your husbands.' We have often failed you:
Lord, forgive us, and help us to obey.]

You have taught us as the Christian family: 'Submit to one another out of reverence for Christ.' We have often failed you:
Lord, forgive us, and help us to obey.

Father, help us all to hear your word, and to obey it; for Jesus' sake. Amen.

6.15   CONFESSION
Editors

Our Father, forgive us this day for times when we fail to honour our parents. Your desire is that we may live in family love and unity: forgive our arrogance and indifference to your commandments. Father of mercy, we put our trust in you:
forgive us and help us.

Forgive us for our anger and the harsh words we sometimes speak to those who are near to us in our family homes. Help us to know your strength as we discipline our tongues. Father of mercy, we put our trust in you:
forgive us and help us.

Forgive us for our unthankful spirit at home; for taking the warmth, comfort and provision as a right, and forgetting that all good gifts come from you. Father of mercy, we put our trust in you:
forgive us and help us for Jesus' sake. Amen.

6.17   COLLECT
Pentecost 14, Church of Ireland APB 1984

God our Father,
your Son Jesus Christ
lived in a family at Nazareth:
grant that in our families on earth
we may so learn to love
    and to live together
that we may rejoice as one family
in your heavenly home;
through Jesus Christ our Lord. **Amen.**

6.18   COLLECT
From Marriage, ASB 1980, adapted

Lord and Saviour Jesus Christ,
who shared at Nazareth
the life of an earthly home:
reign in our homes as Lord and King;
give us grace to serve others
    as you have served us,
and grant that by deed and word
we may be witnesses of your saving love
to those among whom we live;
for the sake of your holy name. **Amen.**

6.19   PSALM
Psalm 128.1–6†

The congregation may divide at A and B

   The pilgrims' song:
A **Blessed are those who fear the Lord,**
B **who walk in his ways.**

→

You will eat the fruit of your work; blessings and prosperity will be yours:

A **Blessed are those who fear the Lord,**
B **who walk in his ways.**

Your wife will be like a fruitful vine within your house; your children will be like young olive trees around your table:

A **Blessed are those who fear the Lord,**
B **who walk in his ways.**

May the Lord bless you all the days of your life; may you have prosperity; may you live to see your children's children:

ALL **Peace be with you. Amen.**

6.24   PRESENTATION OF A BIBLE/ NEW TESTAMENT
Editors

To the father:

It is your responsibility as the father of the family to teach them the word of God:
I will do this, the Lord helping me.

To the mother:

It is your duty as the mother to ensure that your child(ren) shall know the Holy Scriptures:
I will do this, the Lord helping me.

6.25   CREED
From Ephesians 3†

Let us declare our faith in God:

We believe in God the Father,
from whom every family
**   in heaven and on earth**
is named.

We believe in God the Son,
who lives in our hearts through faith,
and fills us with his love.

We believe in God the Holy Spirit,
who strengthens us with power
**   from on high.**

We believe in one God;
Father, Son, and Holy Spirit. Amen.

6.28   FOR OUR MOTHERS
From 'A New Zealand Prayer Book'

Blessed are you,
God of strength and patience;
yours is the love our mothers showed us,
yours the care we need:
as we learn to care for one another
and to share your love,
may it be with our mother
we share it first of all. **Amen.**

6.29   ABOUT A MOTHER'S LOVE
From 'A New Zealand Prayer Book'

Ever–loving God,
your care for us is greater
even than a mother's love for her child;
teach us to value a mother's love
and see in it an expression of your grace,
that we may feel ever more deeply
   your love for us
in Christ Jesus our Saviour. **Amen.**

6.30   FOR OUR FAMILIES
Angela Needham

Lord God, our heavenly Father:
for our families and homes – thank you,
for your love and care – thank you,
for everything you give us – thank you:
make us thoughtful at home,
make us helpful to our parents,
and above all,
teach us to love you more day by day;
for Jesus' sake. **Amen.**

6.35   ABOUT LIVING IN A FAMILY
From 'A New Zealand Prayer Book'

Gentle God,
grant that at home
where we are most truly ourselves,
where we are known at our best
   and worst,
we may learn to forgive and be forgiven.
Amen.

6.36   FOR BLESSING IN A FAMILY
From 'A New Zealand Prayer Book'

God, the Father of us all,
you have created families
    and love of every kind.
Give us courage to listen to each other
and to learn,
and grant us the gentle blessing
    which a home can give. **Amen**.

6.39   DEDICATION
From 1 Samuel 1†

Almighty God,
we present our child, *N*, before you.
We asked you for *him*,
and you granted what we asked of you:
so now we give *him* to you.
For *his* whole life
    he shall be given over to you.
O God, we worship and adore you;
through Jesus, our Lord. **Amen**.

6.44   FOR CHILDREN
Editors

Dear Lord Jesus, hear us as we pray;
bless our children, who are yours too.

We pray for all children who have not
heard of you:
bless them, Lord Jesus.

We pray for all children who cannot see:
bless them, Lord Jesus.

We pray for all children who cannot
hear:
bless them, Lord Jesus.

We pray for all children who cannot
walk:
bless them, Lord Jesus.

We pray for all children who need to take
medicine every day of their lives:
bless them, Lord Jesus.

We pray for all children everywhere who
have special needs:
bless them, Lord Jesus.

Dear Lord Jesus,
hear us as we pray:

bless our children,
who are yours first of all. Amen.

6.45   PARENTS' PRAYER
From 'A New Zealand Prayer Book'

All-embracing God
the hope of every generation,
complete our joy by your presence;
give us quiet strength
    and patient wisdom
as we nurture *N*
in all that is good, and true, and just,
through Jesus Christ
    our friend and brother. **Amen.**

6.54   FOR SAD FAMILIES
Zinnia Bryan

We pray for those who will be unhappy
today:

For mothers who cannot provide for their
children – Lord, in your mercy,
hear our prayer.

For fathers who cannot earn enough
money for their families – Lord, in your
mercy,
hear our prayer.

For children who are ill or frightened –
Lord, in your mercy,
hear our prayer.

For all who are alone, and without
people to love them – Lord, in your
mercy,
hear our prayer.

Bless those who give their lives
in service to the poor and hungry,
and strengthen us to help
    in meeting their needs;
through Jesus Christ our Lord. Amen.

6.57   THANKSGIVING FOR A CHILD
From 'A New Zealand Prayer Book'

We thank you God for this new person,
child of your creation:
may the knowledge of you
    dawn on *him*,

→

may the love of you grow in *him*,
and may the grace of your Spirit
draw *him* to you. **Amen.**

6.59　THANKSGIVING
　　　　FOR OUR FAMILIES
Editors

We thank God for giving us other people
to be part of our lives:

For parents, and the love which brought
us to birth: we praise you, O Lord,
and bring you thanks today.

For mothers who have cherished and
nurtured us: we praise you, O Lord,
and bring you thanks today.

For fathers who have loved and
supported us: we praise you, O Lord,
and bring you thanks today.

For brothers and sisters with whom we
have shared our home: we praise you, O
Lord,
and bring you thanks today.

For children, entrusted to our care as
parents: we praise you, O Lord,
and bring you thanks today.

For other relatives and friends who have
been with us in our hopes and our joys:
we praise you, O Lord,
and bring you thanks today.

For all who first spoke to us of Jesus, and
have drawn us into the family of our
Father in heaven: we praise you, O Lord,
and bring you thanks today.

**Help us to live
as those who belong to one another
　and to you,
now and always. Amen.**

6.60　THANKSGIVING
　　　　FOR OUR FAMILIES
Marjorie Hampson

Thank you, Lord,
for our homes and families,
thank you for our health and happiness,
thank you for the good times,

thank you for helping us to cope
　with the times that are not so good.
Thank you for life itself –
and for your wonderful love
in Jesus Christ our Lord. **Amen.**

6.62　THANKSGIVING FOR FAMILY
　　　　AND FRIENDS
Editors

We thank you, God,
for our family and our friends –
for those who understand us
better than we understand ourselves,
for those who know us at our worst
　and still love us,
for those who have forgiven us
when we had no right
　to expect forgiveness.
Help us to be true to our friends,
as we would expect them to be to us;
through Jesus Christ our Lord. **Amen.**

6.63　THANKSGIVING
　　　　FOR OUR HOMES
Editors

Heavenly Father, we acknowledge you to
be the giver of every good and perfect
gift:

For the homes you have provided for us
as places of rest and refreshment, as
centres of fellowship and friendship:
our God, we thank you.

For the labour and skill of those who
built them, for the comfort of the
amenities provided:
our God, we thank you.

For all the love and affection, the joy and
hope they can bring to those who come
within their walls:
our God, we thank you.

**Be present in our homes –
that no false thing may come there;
bless them with your love –
that your will alone may be done there:
accept our prayer and thanksgiving
through Jesus Christ our Lord. Amen.**

6.64 THANKSGIVING FOR
BLESSINGS OF EVERY AGE
Editors

Dear God, you are our Father; and, whatever our age, we are your children. We thank you for the joy and eagerness of being young, of having boundless energy; we thank you for the fascination of developing skills and faculties of sight, hearing and taste that are sharp and keen. For our early years:
thank you, Father.

We thank you for the years of maturity with their experience and steadiness,

fortitude and hope, that come with proving your goodness. For our middle years:
thank you, Father.

We thank you for the richness of growing old; for the wisdom, the sense of proportion and the humility that age can bring. For our final years:
thank you, Father.

Father, we thank you that,
when our earthly years are spent,
there awaits us life in your presence
with our Lord Jesus Christ. Amen.

Palm Sunday

7.1 GREETING
From Revelation 22†

The grace of the Lord Jesus be with God's people. **Amen.**

7.6 RESPONSE
From Psalm 24†

Fling wide the gates and open the ancient doors:
that the King of glory may come in.

7.7 RESPONSE
From Zechariah 9 and Mark 11†

Shout for joy, you people of Jerusalem! Look, your king is coming to you – triumphant and victorious, but humble and riding on a donkey:
Hosanna!

Blessed is he
who comes in the name of the Lord.
 Amen.

7.8 RESPONSE
From Matthew 21†

Say to the daughter of Zion, 'See, your king comes to you, gentle and riding on a donkey':
Hosanna to the Son of David:
blessed is he
who comes in the name of the Lord.
Hosanna in the highest!

7.9 RESPONSE
From Matthew 21†

Hosanna to the Son of David:
Blessed is he
who comes in the name of the Lord.
Hosanna in the highest!

7.11 PRAISE
From Isaiah 12†

Shout aloud, and sing for joy, people of Zion:
Great is the Holy one of Israel. Amen.

7.12 PRAISE
From Psalm 100†

Shout for joy to the Lord, all the earth;
serve the Lord with gladness!

Come before him with joyful songs;
**give thanks to him and praise his name!
Amen.**

7.13 CONFESSION
Editors

On Palm Sunday, the crowds worshipped
Jesus; on Good Friday they shouted for
him to die. Let us who also worship him,
confess that we sometimes reject him,
and ask his forgiveness:

Lord Jesus Christ, you come to us in
peace, but we shut the door of our mind
against you. In your mercy:
forgive us and help us.

You come to us in humility, but we prefer
our own proud ways. In your mercy:
forgive us and help us.

You come to us in judgement, but we
cling to our familiar sins. In your mercy:
forgive us and help us.

You come to us in majesty, but we will
not have you to reign over us. In your
mercy:
forgive us and help us.

**Lord, forgive our empty praise,
fill our loveless hearts;
come to us
and make our lives your home for ever.
Amen.**

7.14 CONFESSION
From Isaiah 64†

**Sovereign Lord,
we have continually sinned against you;
we have become unclean,
all our righteous acts are like filthy rags;
we shrivel up like leaves,
and our sins sweep us away.
Yet, O Lord, you are our Father:
do not remember our sins for ever.**

**We are your people:
look upon us, we pray,
and forgive us;
through Jesus our redeemer. Amen.**

7.16 COLLECT
Palm Sunday, ASB 1980

Almighty and everlasting God,
who in your tender love
    towards the human race
sent your Son our Saviour Jesus Christ
to take upon him our flesh
and to suffer death upon the cross:
grant that we may follow the example
    of his patience and humility,
and also be made partakers
    of his resurrection;
through Jesus Christ our Lord. **Amen.**

7.17 PSALM
Psalm 24.1–10†

*E – enquirer, D – director, or these lines may
also be said by the minister.*

The earth is the Lord's, and
everything in it:
the world, and all who live here.

He founded it upon the seas:
and established it upon the waters.

E Who has the right to go up the Lord's
hill; who may enter his holy temple?
**Those who have clean hands
and a pure heart,
who do not worship idols
or swear by what is false.**

They receive blessing continually
from the Lord:
**and righteousness
from the God of their salvation.**

Such are the people who seek for God:
**who enter the presence
of the God of Jacob.**

D Fling wide the gates, open the ancient
doors:
that the king of glory may come in.

E Who is the king of glory?
**The Lord, strong and mighty,
the Lord mighty in battle.**

D Fling wide the gates, open the ancient
doors:
that the king of glory may come in.

E Who is he, this king of glory?
**The Lord almighty,
he is the king of glory. Amen.**

7.20 CREED
From Philippians 2†

Let us affirm our faith in Jesus Christ the
Son of God:

**Though he was divine,
he did not cling to equality with God,
but made himself nothing.
Taking the form of a slave,
he became as we are;
as a man he humbled himself,
and was obedient to death –
even the death of the cross.**

**Therefore God has raised him on high,
and given him the name
above every name:
that at the name of Jesus
every knee should bow,
and every voice proclaim
that Jesus Christ is Lord,
to the glory of God the Father. Amen.**

7.21 ADORATION
Based on 1 Corinthians 2†

O Lord, our God:
we worship and adore you.

You have revealed yourself to the simple
and the innocent and have confounded
the arrogant. O Lord, our God:
we worship and adore you.

You have chosen what the world
considers foolish in order to shame the
wise. O Lord, our God:
we worship and adore you.

You have used what the world considers
weak in order to bring down the
powerful. O Lord, our God:
we worship and adore you.

Jesus, Master, entering upon our world,
gentle and majestic, clothed in humility,
riding on a donkey, we acclaim you with
our hosannas. O Lord, our God:
we worship and adore you.

**Blessed is he who comes
in the name of the Lord. Amen.**

7.22 INVITATION
Gordon Bates

Come into our *city*, Lord; bring hope and
a cause for joy. Hosanna to the King
who comes in the name of the Lord!

Come into our *fellowship*, Lord; cleanse it
of all that is not in accordance with your
will. Hosanna to the King
who comes in the name of the Lord!

Come into our hearts, Lord; teach us
your love and your truth. Hosanna to the
King
who comes in the name of the Lord!

**Lord Jesus,
as you entered into Jerusalem
and its Temple,
so come to us
that we may be a holy people,
worthy of your presence,
bringing glory to your name. Amen.**

7.25 THANKSGIVING
After Lancelot Andrewes

Blessing and honour,
thanksgiving and praise,
more than we can utter,
more than we can conceive,
be to your glorious name, O God,
Father, Son and Holy Spirit,
by all angels, all people, all creation,
for ever and ever. **Amen.**

Passiontide, Good Friday, Easter Eve

8.1 GREETING
From Galatians 1†

Grace and peace be with you from God our Father and the Lord Jesus Christ, who gave himself for our sins according to the will of our God and Father; to whom be glory for ever and ever. **Amen.**

8.12 RESPONSE
From 2 Corinthians 5†

Jesus died for all:
**that we who live
should no longer live for ourselves
but for him who for our sake died
and was raised to life. Amen.**

8.13 RESPONSE
From Ephesians 2†

You who once were far away have been brought near through the blood of Christ:
he himself is our peace!

8.14 RESPONSE
From Romans 5†

God demonstrates his own love for us in this:
**while we were still sinners,
Christ died for us.**

8.17 CONFESSION
From Psalm 143†

**O Lord, we have let you down,
darkness overtakes us,
our spirits fail
and our hearts are dismayed;
your face is hidden from us
and we wait for your word of love:
hear our prayer,
listen to our cry for mercy;
in your faithfulness and righteousness
come to our relief;
do not bring us to judgement –
for no-one living
  is righteous before you;**

**show us the way we should go,
teach us to do your will
and let your Spirit lead us;
through Jesus Christ our Lord. Amen.**

8.18 CONFESSION
Editors

Lord Jesus, we feel the burden of Good Friday, for we know that on this day you suffered, bled and died for us. For our sin:
Lord, forgive us.

In our weakness:
Lord, strengthen us.

We are totally unable to earn or merit your forgiveness and your renewing love. We can only recall with wonder your sacrifice, and seek you with penitence and faith. For our sin:
Lord, forgive us.

In our weakness:
Lord, strengthen us.

We so often fail you and betray you – by our silence, by our neglect, and in our fear of being hurt. For our sin:
Lord, forgive us.

In our weakness:
Lord, strengthen us.

We confess our disobedience and our spirit of neglect. Help us not to shirk our duty to bear your cross, or seek to avoid our responsibilities as your redeemed in the world. For our sin:
Lord, forgive us.

In our weakness:
Lord, strengthen us.

**Cleanse us from our sin
by your precious blood,
and graciously restore us
  to your service
for your glory and your praise. Amen.**

8.21 PRAISE
From Psalm 103†

Praise the Lord and do not forget his blessings:
**he heals our diseases
and rescues our life from hell.**

He crowns us with love and compassion:
he satisfies us with good things.

Praise the Lord! Amen.

8.22 CONFESSION
Editors

Lord Jesus Christ, we confess we have failed you as did your disciples, and we ask for your mercy and your help:

When we are tempted to betray you for the sake of selfish gain: Christ, have mercy;
Lord, forgive us and help us.

When we do not keep watch in prayer, and will not share the pain of your suffering: Christ, have mercy;
Lord, forgive us and help us.

When we allow the world to silence you, and run away from those who abuse you: Christ, have mercy;
Lord, forgive us and help us.

When we will not confess your name, and fear the consequences of being known to belong to you: Christ, have mercy;
Lord, forgive us and help us.

When we spurn your dying love, and will not offer you the sacrifice of our lives: Christ, have mercy:
Lord, forgive us and help us.

**Cleanse us from our sins
by your precious blood,
and graciously restore us to your service;
for your praise and glory. Amen.**

8.23 COLLECT
Good Friday, ASB 1980

Almighty Father,
look with mercy on this your family
for which our Lord Jesus Christ
was content to be betrayed
and given up into the hands
of the wicked,
and to suffer death upon the cross;
who is alive and glorified
with you and the Holy Spirit,
one God, now and for ever. **Amen.**

8.24 PSALM
From Psalm 22†

I am poured out like water, and all my bones are out of joint; my heart has turned to wax – it has melted away within me. My strength is dried up and my tongue sticks to the roof of my mouth; you lay me in the dust of death. Dogs have surrounded me; a band of evil men has encircled me, they have pierced my hands and my feet. I can count all my bones; people stare and gloat over me. They divide my garments among them and cast lots for my clothing. But you, O Lord, be not far off; O my strength, come quickly to help me.
**All the ends of the earth will remember
and turn to the Lord,
and all the families of the nations
will bow down before him,
for dominion belongs to the Lord
and he rules over the nations.**

My God, my God, why have you forsaken me? Why are you so far from saving me, so far from the words of my groaning? O my God, I cry out by day, but you do not answer, by night, and am not silent. Yet you are enthroned as the Holy One; you are the praise of Israel.
**In you our fathers put their trust;
they trusted and you delivered them.
They cried to you and were saved;
in you they trusted
and were not disappointed.**

But I am a worm and not a man, scorned by men and despised by the people. All who see me mock me; they hurl insults, shaking their heads:
**He trusts in the Lord –
let the Lord rescue him;
let him deliver him
since he delights in him!**

Posterity will serve him, future
generations will be told about the Lord:
they will proclaim his righteousness
to a people yet unborn
for he has saved us. Amen.

8.25   CANTICLE
From Isaiah 53†

The people reply:
Who has believed our message:
to whom
has the arm of the Lord been revealed?

He grew up before him like a tender
shoot:
and like a root out of dry ground.

He was despised and rejected:
a man of sorrows
and familiar with grief.

Surely he took up our infirmities:
and carried our sorrows.

He was pierced for our transgressions;
he was crushed for our iniquities.

The punishment that brought us peace
was upon him:
and by his wounds we are healed.

He was led like a lamb to the slaughter,
and as a sheep before her shearers is
silent:
so he did not open his mouth.

He was assigned a grave with the
wicked:
and with the rich in his death.

We all, like sheep have gone astray;
each of us has turned to our own way:
and the Lord has laid on him
the iniquity of us all. Amen.

8.27   CREED
From Galatians 2†

We have been crucified with Christ
and we no longer live,
but Christ lives in us.
The life we live in the body
we live by faith in the Son of God,
who loved us and gave himself for us.
Amen.

8.28   CREED
From 1 Peter 3†

Let us confess our faith in Christ:

Christ died for sins
once for all,
the just for the unjust,
to bring us to God:
he was put to death in the body,
but made alive by the Spirit;
he has gone up on high,
and is at God's right hand,
ruling over angels
and the powers of heaven. Amen.

8.29   FOR JESUS HELP:
A PERSONAL PRAYER
From 'A New Zealand Prayer Book'

Your cross, Jesus,
remains like a tree on a hill:
you show me where I am,
you take away my fear,
and set me on my course again;
help me to watch for you night and day.
Amen.

8.30   FOR THOSE IN NEED
Alan Warren, adapted

Lord Christ,
shine upon all who are in the darkness
     of suffering or grief,
that in your light
they may receive hope and courage,
in your mercy obtain relief and comfort,
and in your presence
find their rest and peace;
for your love's sake. **Amen.**

8.35   ABOUT SELF-SACRIFICE
Alan Gaunt

Living God,
whose Son died on the cross
     for everyone who lives:
show us by his dying
how the place of defeat
can be the place of victory;
and help us to take up our own cross
whatever form it takes,

so that women and men
may recognise your love in us
and come to you, with Christ,
in Resurrection glory. **Amen.**

8.38 PRAYER OF REFLECTION
Based on Matthew 26 and 27, Editors

'Greetings, master!'. Lord, deliver us
from Judas' duplicity – follower until the
going was rough and the money ran out.
Grant us an obedience which seeks the
eternal kingdom. 'Greetings, master!' In
your service:
Lord, make us faithful.

'Do we need any more witnesses?' Lord,
deliver us from the High Priest's
deviousness, following prejudice in the
name of piety. Grant us a religion open to
the Spirit and full of love. 'Do we need
any more witnesses?' In our religion:
Lord, make us honest.

'I do not know the man!' Lord, deliver us
from Peter's denial – following at a
distance until the human cost became too
great. Grant us a courage which will not
hesitate to acknowledge our master. 'I do
not know the man!' In our discipleship:
Lord, make us true.

'What shall I do with him?' Lord, deliver
us from Pilate's dereliction of duty,
following neither truth nor the
promptings of conscience. Grant us a
social awareness that does not wash its
hands of justice. 'What shall I do with
him?' In our care for others:
Lord, make us merciful.

For Jesus' sake. Amen.

8.40 FOR OURSELVES
Salvator mundi

O Saviour of the world,
by your cross and precious blood,
you have redeemed us:
**Save us and help us,
we humbly beseech you, O Lord. Amen.**

8.41 INTERCESSION
ON EASTER EVE
Editors

Lord Jesus, we pray this night for all who
look for your light, for all who have no
hope in this world, for those who have
rejected you, and for those who have
denied you. Lord in your mercy:
hear our prayer.

We pray this night for all who are tired
or hungry, for all who are anxious or ill,
for those who are afraid of dying, and for
those who do not believe in the
resurrection from the dead. Lord in your
mercy:
hear our prayer.

We pray this night for all who trust/*are
baptized* in you, for the fellowship of
those we love, for all in other lands who
celebrate his rising, and for those who are
persecuted for their faith. Lord in your
mercy:
hear our prayer.

**Lord Jesus, on this night
we lift to you our hands and our hearts,
looking for the dawn of a new day
and the everlasting hope of heaven
in the faith of your resurrection. Amen.**

8.43 THANKSGIVING
Editors

O God our Father, you loved the world
so much that you sent your only Son to
die that we might live through him.

('Forgive them . . . ') For Jesus'
willingness to forgive in the face of bitter
hatred, Father, we thank you,
and praise your holy name.

('Today you shall be with me in
paradise.') For Jesus' promise of heaven
to the forgiven sinner, Father, we thank
you,
and praise your holy name.

('Mother . . . behold your son.') For the
example of Jesus' compassion to the last,
Father, we thank you,
and praise your holy name.

('I thirst . . . ') For Jesus' sharing in our physical suffering and longing, Father, we thank you,
and praise your holy name.

('Why have you forsaken me?') For Jesus' entering into our mental suffering and loneliness, Father, we thank you,
and praise your holy name.

('It is finished?') For the completion of Jesus' saving work, and for the covenant of love between God and his world, Father, we thank you,
and praise your holy name.

('Into your hands I commit my spirit.') For Jesus' triumph over death and the certainty of eternal life, Father, we thank you,
and praise your holy name.

Father, God, as you loved us,
so by your grace
help us to love one another,
through Jesus Christ our Lord. Amen.

8.46   THANKSGIVING
Richard of Chichester adapted

Thanks be to you, Lord Jesus Christ,
for all the cruel pains and insults
    you have borne for us;
for all the many blessings
    you have won for us.
Holy Jesus,
most merciful Redeemer,
    friend and brother,

may we know you more clearly,
love you more dearly,
and follow you more nearly,
day by day. **Amen.**

8.47   DEDICATION
Editors

Lord, draw us to your Cross which brings forgiveness:
that we may be cleansed.

Lord, draw us to your Cross which brings light:
that we may have vision.

Lord, draw us to your Cross which brings love:
that we may have compassion.

Lord, draw us to your Cross which brings Life:
that we may live for you.

Lord, draw us to yourself
and to each other;
one Body in heaven and on earth. Amen.

8.48   ASCRIPTION
From Revelation 1†

To him who loves us,
and has freed us from our sins
    by his blood,
and has made us to be a kingdom
    and priests
to serve his God and Father –
to him be glory and power
for ever and ever. **Amen.**

Easter, Resurrection

9.1   GREETING
From Revelation 1†

Grace and peace to you from Jesus Christ, who is the faithful witness, the first-born from the dead. **Amen.**

9.2   GREETING
From Revelation 1† (alternative)

Grace and peace to you from God who is, and who was, and who is to come, and from Jesus Christ, the faithful witness, the first-born from the dead. **Amen.**

9.9 RESPONSE
From Romans 6†

Christ raised from the dead will never die again:
death no longer has power over him: Alleluia!

9.10 RESPONSE
From Luke 24†

Why do you look for the living among the dead?
He is not here, he is risen!

9.11 RESPONSE
From Acts 2†

God has raised this Jesus to life:
we are all witnesses.

9.12 RESPONSE
From 2 Corinthians 1†

All God's promises are 'Yes!' in Christ, and through him we reply 'Amen', to the glory of God: **Amen.**

9.13 RESPONSE
From 2 Corinthians 13†

In weakness Christ was put to death on the Cross:
by God's power he lives!

9.14 RESPONSE
From Romans 7†

Who will rescue us from this body of death?
**Thanks be to God –
through Jesus Christ our Lord!**

9.15 RESPONSE
From Galatians 5†

Freedom is ours:
**Christ has set us free.
Alleluia! Amen.**

9.16 RESPONSE
From 1 Peter 1†

Praise be to the God and Father of our Lord Jesus Christ!

**In his great mercy he has given us
new birth into a living hope
through the resurrection of Jesus Christ
from the dead. Amen.**

9.17 RESPONSE
Frank Colquhoun, adapted

We are risen with Christ –
the Lord is risen!

Eternal life is ours –
the Lord is risen!

Death has met its master –
the Lord is risen!

The way to heaven is open –
the Lord is risen!

He is risen indeed –
Alleluia! Amen.

9.18 APPROACH
Editors

Our God and Father, as this new morning breaks, and there dawns the full light of another Resurrection day, we have come to worship you. In your presence we begin to understand the energy of your Spirit and the power of your love. Our hearts are warmed again, and you renew our confidence. Heavenly Father, on Easter Day:
we praise and adore you.

Lord Jesus, Easter morning tells us that you are alive; that nothing can separate us from your love. We join the countless number in heaven and on earth who proclaim your victory. Risen Lord Jesus, nothing can hold you now from fulfilling your work on earth through your Church. Lord Jesus, Saviour, on Easter Day:
we praise and adore you.

Holy Spirit of God, we come to renew our hearts and minds so that in daily contact with those who know our friendship, or share our place of employment, or live with us in the intimacy of our homes, we may realise our partnership with you: meeting the needs of the world with the power of Jesus' Resurrection. Holy Spirit of God, on Easter Day:
we praise and adore you.

O Lord our God,
Father, Son and Holy Spirit,
yours is the kingdom,
the power and the glory,
for ever and ever. Amen.

9.19 PRAISE
From Psalm 86†

O Lord our God,
we will praise you with all our heart.

O Lord our God,
we will proclaim your greatness
for ever.

Great is your constant love for us;
you have saved us from the grave itself!
Amen.

9.20 CONFESSION
Alternative Confession, ASB 1980

Almighty God, our heavenly Father,
we have sinned against you,
through our own fault,
in thought and word and deed,
and in what we have left undone.
For your Son
our Lord Jesus Christ's sake,
forgive us all that is past;
and grant that we may serve you
in newness of life
to the glory of your name. Amen.

9.21 CONFESSION
Editors

O Jesus Christ, risen master and triumphant Lord, we bow before you in sorrow for our sins, and confess to you our weakness and unbelief:

We have lived by our own strength, and not by the power of your resurrection. In your mercy, forgive us:
Lord, hear us and help us.

We have lived by the light of our own eyes, as faithless and not believing. In your mercy, forgive us:
Lord, hear us and help us.

We have lived for this world alone, and doubted our home in heaven. In your mercy, forgive us:
Lord, hear us and help us.

Lift our minds above earthly things,
set them on things in heaven;
show us your glory and your power,
that we may serve you gladly
all our days. Amen.

9.23 COLLECT
9 before Easter ASB, ASB 1980

Eternal God,
whose Son Jesus Christ is for all people
the way, the truth and the life:
grant us to walk in his way,
to rejoice in his truth,
and to share his risen life;
who is alive and reigns with you
and the Holy Spirit,
one God, now and for ever. **Amen.**

9.24 COLLECT
Easter, ASB 1980

Lord of all life and power,
who through the mighty resurrection
of your Son
overcame the old order of sin and death
to make all things new in him:
grant that we,
being dead to sin and alive to you
in Jesus Christ,

may reign with him in glory;
to whom with you and the Holy Spirit
be praise and honour, glory and might,
now and in all eternity. **Amen.**

9.25 PSALM
Psalm 126.1–6†

When the Lord brought us back from
slavery:
we were like those who dream.

Our mouths were filled with laughter:
our tongues with songs of joy.

Then those around us said, 'The Lord has
done great things for them':
**The Lord has done great things for us,
and we are filled with joy.**

Those who sow in tears
shall reap with songs of joy. Amen.

9.30 CREED
From 1 Corinthians 15†

Let us declare our faith in the
resurrection of our Lord Jesus Christ:

**Christ died for our sins
in accordance with the scriptures;
he was buried;
he was raised to life on the third day
in accordance with the scriptures;
afterwards he appeared to his followers,
and to all the apostles:
this we have received,
and this we believe. Amen.**

9.31 CREED
From 1 Peter 1, Romans 4 and 8†

Let us proclaim our faith:

**We believe in God the Father,
by whose great mercy
we have been born again
to a living hope,
through the ressurection
    of Jesus Christ
from the dead.**

**We believe in God the Son,
who died for our sin,
and rose again for our justification.**

**We believe in God the Holy Spirit,
who bears witness with our spirit
that we are the children of God.**

**We believe in one God:
Father, Son, and Holy Spirit. Amen.**

9.32 FOR JESUS' PRESENCE AND POWER
Michael Bolting, adapted

Lord Jesus, our risen Saviour,
we rejoice in your mighty victory
    over sin and death:
you are the Prince of Life;
you are alive for evermore.
Help us to know your presence
    in our worship,
and to receive your power in our lives;
until we rise to live with you for ever.
Amen.

9.33 FOR THE CHURCH
Editors

O God, our Father,
we give you thanks for our Church:
shed the light of your Holy Spirit here,
that all who enter in may find you.
Bless us with your presence;
let love reach out and be met with love,
rest your hand
    on all who minister for you;
for the sake of Jesus,
our Saviour and risen Lord. **Amen.**

9.34 FOR FAITH
David Silk

Grant to us, Lord God,
to trust you not for ourselves alone,
but for those also whom we love
and who are hidden from us
by the shadow of death;
that, as we believe your power
to have raised our Lord Jesus Christ
    from the dead,

→

so we may trust your love
to give eternal life
   to all who believe in him;
through Jesus Christ our Lord,
who is alive and reigns with you
   and the Holy Spirit,
one God, now and for ever. **Amen.**

9.35   FOR OUR FAITH
Editors

Gracious Father, God of Love,
we rejoice in the glorious resurrection
of your Son, Jesus Christ;
we praise you and thank you
   for our Saviour,
who triumphed over death
to reign as Lord of life.
Strengthen us, Father;
grant us a firm faith,
that we may know the presence of Jesus
our Wonderful Counsellor
   and true friend:
all glory and honour to his name! **Amen.**

9.37   THANKSGIVING
Editors

We give thanks to our Lord Jesus Christ
for the hope of Easter:

For your penetrating love which has
pierced the darkness and redeemed the
utter despair of humanity, we give you
thanks, Lord Jesus.
We praise you, risen Christ.

That you have taken our sorrows, our
failure and our weakness and have
transformed them by the power and
radiance of your resurrection, we give
you thanks, Lord Jesus.
We praise you, risen Christ.

For your church, to whom you have
given the message of reconciliation to
proclaim to the world, we give you
thanks, Lord Jesus.
We praise you, risen Christ.

Alleluia! Amen.

9.38   THANKSGIVING
Richard Hughes

Our Lord Jesus Christ, risen from death,
we praise you for changed lives and new
hopes at Easter:

You came to Mary in the garden, and
turned her tears into joy. For your love
and your mercy:
we give you thanks, O Lord.

You came to the disciples in the upper
room, and turned their fear into courage.
For your love and your mercy:
we give you thanks, O Lord.

You came to the disciples by the lakeside,
and turned their failure into faith. For
your love and your mercy:
we give you thanks, O Lord.

You came to the disciples on the
Emmaus road, and turned their despair
into hope. For your love and your mercy:
we give you thanks, O Lord.

You come to us in our unworthiness and
shame, and turn our weakness into
triumph. For your love and your mercy:
we give you thanks, O Lord.

Lord Jesus,
wherever there are tears,
or fear, or failure,
or despair, or weakness:
come, reveal to us
your love, your mercy,
   and your risen power;
for the glory of your name.
Alleluia! Amen.

9.39   THANKSGIVING
From 1 Peter 1†

Praise be to you, O God our Father:
for in your great mercy
you have given us new birth
into a living hope
through the resurrection from the dead
of Jesus Christ our Lord. **Amen.**

9.41 RESURRECTION
THANKSGIVING
From 'New Every Morning', adapted

Because you have broken for us the chains of sin and brought us into fellowship with our heavenly Father:
thanks be to you, our Lord Jesus Christ.

Because you overcame death and opened for us the gates of eternal life:
thanks be to you, our Lord Jesus Christ.

Because when two or three gather in your name you are present with them:
thanks be to you, our Lord Jesus Christ.

Because you ever live to intercede for us:
thanks be to you, our Lord Jesus Christ.

**For these and all other benefits
of your glorious resurrection,
thanks be to you, Lord Jesus Christ.
Amen.**

9.42 EASTER COMMISSION
From John 21†

Jesus asks each one of us, 'Do you truly love me?'
Yes, Lord, you know that I love you.

'Feed my lambs'. Jesus asks us each by name, 'Do you truly love me?'
Yes, Lord, you know that I love you.

'Take care of my sheep'. Jesus asks us the third time, 'Do you love me?'
**Lord, you know all things,
you know that I love you.**

Jesus tells us, 'Feed my sheep! Follow me!'
Amen.

God's Creation

10.1 GREETING
From 1 Peter 1†

Grace and peace be yours in full measure. **Amen.**

10.7 RESPONSE
From Genesis 1†

God saw all that he had made:
it was very good.

10.8 RESPONSE
From Psalm 19†

The heavens declare the glory of God:
**the skies proclaim
the work of his hands.**

10.9 RESPONSE
From Isaiah 45†

The Lord who created the heavens, who fashioned and made the earth:
he is God!

10.10 RESPONSE
From Psalm 8†

O Lord, our Lord:
**how majestic is your name
in all the earth!**

10.11 INVITATION
From Nehemiah 9†

Stand up and praise the Lord your God,
who is from everlasting.

Blessed be his glorious name, let it be exalted above all blessing and praise:
Stand up and praise the Lord your God,
who is from everlasting.

→

He alone is the Lord, he made the highest heavens and all their starry host, the earth and all that is on it, the seas and all that is in them: Stand up and praise the Lord your God,
who is from everlasting.

He gives life to everything, and the multitudes of heaven worship him: Stand up and praise the Lord your God,
who is from everlasting.

We praise you O God
for you have created all things
and made us anew
in Jesus Christ our Lord. Amen.

10.12 INVITATION
From Song of Songs 2†

See, the winter is past:
the snows are over and gone.

Flowers appear on the earth:
the season of singing has come.

The trees are beginning to bud:
the blossom has spread its fragrance.

The cry of the birds is heard in our land. Arise, come and worship. **Amen.**

10.14 APPROACH
Editors

Gracious God and creator, the variety of beauty and colour in the world often leaves us speechless; the rolling hills, the mighty seas, the desert plains and the succulent green pastures, all proclaim your power and creative provision. O Lord our God:
we praise and adore you.

We praise you for the warming sun, the growth-making rain, the freshness of a new morning and the calm of a still evening: all proclaim your purpose and your pleasure. O Lord our God:
we praise and adore you.

We praise you for your Son, our Saviour, Jesus Christ: through him we have received pardon for our sin and the joy of salvation; for he lived and died and rose again to redeem us. O Lord our God:
we praise and adore you.

For all the work of your hands,
and for every gift
  from your heart of love,
we exalt your holy name
for ever and ever. Amen.

10.15 PRAISE
From Psalm 8†

O Lord our God, how glorious is your name in all the earth:
high above the heavens
your majesty is praised. Amen.

10.16 CONFESSION
From 'Worship Now'

Almighty God, we confess that we have often misused and ill-treated your creation: hear us, and in your mercy save us and help us.

For every act of carelessness that has treated the world merely as a playground: Father, forgive us –
save us and help us.

For every act of wastefulness that forgets the crying of the needy: Father, forgive us –
save us and help us.

For every act of selfishness that defies your just rule over our lives: Father, forgive us –
save us and help us.

Cleanse us from our sins
through the love of Christ,
and set us free for his service
through the power of the Spirit;
for the glory of your name. Amen.

10.17 CONFESSION
From Psalm 106†

O Lord our God,
we have not obeyed your commands,
we have not always done what is right;
we have sinned
  through our human nature,
we have done wrong
and acted wickedly;
we have forgotten
  your many kindnesses
and we have rebelled against you:
O Lord, forgive us and save us
bring us back and restore us;
that we may give thanks
  to your holy name
and glory in your praise. Amen.

10.19 COLLECT
Rogation Days, ASB 1980

Almighty God,
you have provided
the resources of the world
to maintain the life of your children,
and have so ordered our life
that we are dependent upon each other.
Bless us all in our daily work
and, as you have given us
  the knowledge to produce plenty
so give us the will
to bring it within reach of all;
through Jesus Christ our Lord. **Amen.**

10.21 PSALM
Psalm 67.1–7†

The congregation may divide at A and B

May God be gracious to us and bless
us:
A **and make his face to shine upon us.**

Let your ways be known upon earth:
B **your saving grace to every nation.**

Let the peoples praise you, O God:
ALL **let the peoples praise you.**

Let the nations be glad:
A **and sing aloud for joy.**

Because you judge the peoples
justly:
B **and guide the nations of the earth.**

Let the peoples praise you, O God:
ALL **let all the peoples praise you.**

Then the land will yield its harvest:
A **and God, our God, will bless us.**

God will bless us:
B **and people will fear him**
ALL **to the ends of the earth. Amen.**

10.22 PSALM
Psalm 148. 1–14†

The congregation may divide at A and B

Praise the Lord!

Praise the Lord from the heavens:
praise him in the heights above.

Praise him, all his angels:
A **praise him, all his heavenly host.**

Praise him, sun and moon:
B **praise him, all you shining stars.**

Let them praise the name of the
Lord:
ALL **Praise the Lord!**

Praise the Lord from the earth:
A **praise him, great sea creatures.**

Praise him, storms and clouds:
B **praise him, mountains and hills.**

Praise him, fields and woods:
A **praise him, animals and birds.**

Praise him, rulers and nations:
B **praise him, old and young.**

Let them praise the name of the
Lord:
ALL **Praise the Lord! Amen.**

10.24 CREED
From Isaiah 44†

We believe in one God
who made all things;
he alone stretched out the heavens
and spread out the earth:
he formed us in the womb.

→

He is our king and our redeemer –
the Lord almighty.

We belong to the Lord –
we are his people
and are called by his name;
he pours out his Spirit upon us
as water on a thirsty land.

We believe in one God, the almighty,
Father, Son and Holy Spirit. Amen.

10.25   CREED
From Isaiah 44†

We believe in one God who made all
things:

Did he stretch out the heavens,
spread out the earth, and form us in the
womb?
He did!

Is he the Lord almighty, our king and
redeemer?
He is!

Are we his own people, called by his
name?
We are!

Does he pour his Spirit on us as on a dry
and thirsty land?
He does!

We believe in one God, the Almighty,
Father Son and Holy Spirit.
Amen.

10.26   CREED
From Colossians 1†

Christ is the image of the invisible God,
the first-born over all creation.
By him all things were created:
things in heaven and on earth,
visible and invisible;
all things were created
by him and for him.
He is before all things
and in him all things hold together.
He is the head of the body, the Church;
he is the beginning and the first-born
   from among the dead. Amen.

10.28   FOR FORGIVENESS
Alan Gaunt

For our misuse of the world, our wanton
destruction of life and our thoughtless
pollution of the atmosphere:
Lord, forgive us.

For our greed of gain, our poverty of
spirit and our lust for power:
Lord, forgive us.

For our loss of nerve, our lapses into
despair, and our failure to unite the
human family:
Lord, forgive us,
for the sake of Jesus Christ our Saviour.
Amen.

10.29   ABOUT OURSELVES
AND GOD'S CREATION
Michael Botting

Lord of the universe,
we praise you for your creation;
for the wonder of space,
the beauty of the world
and the value of earth's resources:
keep us from spoiling these your gifts
   by our selfishness
and help us to use them
   for the good of all people
and the glory of your name. Amen.

10.33   FOR OURSELVES
From 'Prayers and Hymns for Junior Schools'

O Lord,
open our eyes to see what is beautiful,
our minds to know what is true,
and our hearts to love what is good;
for Jesus' sake. Amen.

10.38   THANKSGIVING
FOR OUR SENSES
Editors

O Lord of love and creation, we thank you
for the privilege and blessing of living in a
world filled with beauty, excitement and
variety:

For the gift of loving and being loved, for

friendship and understanding, we lift up our hearts:
and give you our thanks, O Lord.

For the beauty of forests and marshes, for the green of meadows and trees, we lift up our hearts:
and give you our thanks, O Lord.

For the sound of waterfalls and rippling streams, for the happy cries of children and the interest they bring, we lift up our hearts:
and give you our thanks, O Lord.

For the delight of music and words, for the stimulus of others' thoughts and conversation, for books to read – by the fireside, or in bed with the rain falling on the roof or the snow blowing past outside the window – we lift up our hearts:
and give you our thanks, O Lord.

For all your providence and generosity, we thank you, O Lord our God. Amen.

10.39 GENERAL THANKSGIVING
From 'Contemporary Prayers for Public Worship', adapted

Let us thank God for all his goodness to us:

For creating the world and for preserving it until now: we give you thanks, O Lord,
and praise your holy name.

For the regular return of day and night, and of the seasons: we give you thanks, O Lord,
and praise your holy name.

For the wonder of nature and the beauty of the earth: we give you thanks, O Lord,
and praise your holy name.

For our memory, which enables us to build on the experience of the past: we give you thanks, O Lord,
and praise your holy name.

For our imagination, which admits us to a wider world than we could otherwise know: we give you thanks, O Lord,
and praise your holy name.

For the grace by which you have revealed yourself to us: we give you thanks, O Lord,
and praise your holy name.

For your patience with our waywardness and your forgiveness for our sinfulness: we give you thanks, O Lord,
and praise your holy name.

**Above all we thank you
for the promise of all things made new,
and for our re-creation in your dear Son,
Jesus Christ our Lord. Amen.**

10.41 PRAISE FOR CREATION
Editors

Our God and Father, we praise you for everything that ministers to us in your wonderful world.

For the inspiration of morning mists:
our God, we praise you.

For the dew on field and flower:
our God, we praise you.

For the whispering wind and purifying rain:
our God, we praise you.

For sunshine, warmth and colour:
our God, we praise you.

For the calm seas reflecting the beauty of skies:
our God, we praise you.

For the flying spume and the lashing waves that speak of your power and might:
our God, we praise you.

**For all that we see
in the world around us,
we praise you,
in Jesus' name, Amen.**

10.42 PRAISE FOR ALL GOD'S GIFTS
Edward Smalley

For creation with its order and beauty; for the rhythm of the seasons – summer,

winter, spring, and autumn – and for all that sustains our life on earth: our God we thank you,
and bring you praise today.

For all that makes the earth our home; for other people whose labours and skills contribute to our needs, for institutions of society which provide for our health and security: our God we thank you,
and bring you praise today.

For families and the love of partners, for our parents and our children, for the concern and interest of those who anticipate our needs and provide for our well-being, for the loyalty of friends and all who encourage and sustain us by their words and examples: our God we thank you,
and bring you praise today.

For work and leisure, hobbies and sport; for literature, music and art, radio and television, and for every medium by which we draw upon the treasury of others' thoughts: our God we thank you,
and bring you praise today.

For the Christian church with its opportunities of friendship, service and worship, for the communion of saints; for your word of life in Jesus our Lord, for the Holy Spirit ever present to guide and to enable; for the hope of heaven and for life eternal: our God we thank you,
and bring you praise today.

(Especially for . . . : our God we thank you,
and bring you praise today.)

Praise the Lord:
praise his holy name. Amen.

10.43 ASCRIPTION
Jim Cotter

To God the Creator,
who loved us first
and gave this world to be our home;
to God the Redeemer,
who loves us
and by dying and rising
pioneered the way of freedom;
to God the Sanctifier,
who spreads the divine love in our hearts,
be praise and glory for time
    and for eternity. **Amen.**

10.44 ASCRIPTION
From Nehemiah 9†

Blessed be your glorious name,
O Lord our God;
may it be exalted
above all human worship and praise.
You alone are the Lord,
you made the skies
and the universe beyond;
you made the earth and all that is on it,
the sea and all that is in it;
you give life to everything.
You are the Lord our God;
with the hosts of heaven
    we worship you. **Amen.**

10.45 DOXOLOGY
Thomas Ken, adapted

Praise God
    from whom all blessings flow,
in heaven above and earth below;
one God, three persons, we adore –
to him be praise for evermore! **Amen.**

10.46 DOXOLOGY
From Psalm 63†

Lord God, our God,
we have seen you in the sanctuary,
we have looked on your power
    and your glory.
Because your love is better than life
our lips will glorify you,
we will praise you as long as we live,
and in your name
    we will lift up our hearts;
through Jesus Christ our Lord. **Amen**

Jesus is Lord, Ascension

11.1 GREETING
From 2 Timothy 1†

Grace, mercy and peace from God the Father and Christ Jesus our Lord. **Amen.**

11.7 RESPONSE
From Acts 2 and Philippians 2†

Be assured of this – God has made this Jesus both Lord and Christ:
**God has exalted him,
and given him
a name above every name. Amen.**

11.8 RESPONSE
From Revelation 11†

We give you thanks, Lord God Almighty, the One who is and who was, because you have taken your great power and have begun to reign. **Amen.**

11.9 RESPONSE
From Revelation 11†

The kingdom of this world has become the kingdom of our Lord and of his Christ:
**and he will reign for ever and ever.
Amen.**

11.10 RESPONSE
From Revelation 12†

Now have come the salvation and the power and the kingdom of our God, and the authority of his Christ:
Amen.

11.11 APPROACH
From 'Companion to the Lectionary', adapted

God our Father, King of heaven:
**all honour and glory and power
are yours by right.**

Jesus Christ, crucified, risen, ascended Lord:
**all honour and glory and power
are yours by right.**

Spirit of God, lighting upon us, filling our lives with love, spurring us to greater deeds:
**all honour and glory and power
are yours by right.**

Our glorious and holy God, we praise you for all that makes the unseen heaven a reality to us while we live on earth: for word and sacrament, for faithful Christians past and present, for fellowship in the Church, and for times of deep awareness that Jesus is with us always.
**One God, Father, Son and Holy Spirit:
all honour and glory and power
are yours by right. Amen.**

11.12 PRAISE
From Psalm 68†

Sing to God, O kingdoms of the earth;
sing praises to the Lord!

Sing to God, O kingdoms of the earth;
proclaim his mighty power!

Praise the Lord! **Amen.**

11.13 CONFESSION
Editors

**Lord Jesus Christ,
crucified, risen and ascended for us:
we have not loved you as our Redeemer,
nor obeyed you as our Lord;
we have not brought our prayers to you,
nor heeded your tears
    shed over the world.
Forgive us, we pray;
breathe into us a new spirit of service,
and make us joyfully obedient
    to your will:
for your glory's sake. Amen.**

11.14 CONFESSION/PRAYER FOR
          FORGIVENESS
Editors

For our failure to appreciate and enjoy
the good things you provide for our
lives, in your mercy:
Lord, forgive us.

For our insensitivity to the needs of
others, and for our over-sensitivity when
we are hurt by them, in your mercy:
Lord, forgive us.

For becoming consumed in the business
of life, and for losing faith in your
sovereignty and power, in your mercy:
Lord, forgive us.

For moods of disobedience and for
outright rejection of your will, in your
mercy:
Lord, forgive us.

For consenting to wrong practices by our
cool silence, and for listening to scandal,
in your mercy:
Lord, forgive us.

**Reform our will,
reinforce our courage:
create in us a new heart, O God,
and put your righteousness in us;
through Jesus Christ our Lord. Amen.**

11.15 CONFESSION
From 'Lamentations 5†

**Remember, O Lord,
your people in their sorrow;
look, and see our disgrace:
joy is gone from our hearts;
our dancing has turned to mourning,
we are no longer proud –
the crown has fallen from our head –
for we have sinned.
You, O Lord, reign for ever,
your throne endures
    to every generation:
do not forget us now,
do not forsake us for long:
forgive us, restore us and renew us
through our redeemer
    Jesus Christ. Amen.**

11.17 COLLECT
John Austin, adapted

O God,
you have exalted the crucified Saviour
    your Son
by a triumphant resurrection
    and ascension into heaven.
May his triumphs and glories
so shine in our hearts and minds,
that we may be able to understand
    more readily
his sufferings,
and more courageously face our own;
through Jesus Christ our Lord
who, with you and the Spirit
lives and reigns,
one God for ever and ever. **Amen.**

11.18 PSALM
Psalm 47.1–9†

The congregation may divide at A and B

Clap your hands, all you nations:
shout to God with cries of joy.

How awesome is the Lord most
high:
A **the King who rules
    the whole wide earth!**

God has ascended to his throne:
B **with shouts of joy
    and sound of trumpets.**

Sing praises to our God, sing praises:
A **sing praises to our King,
    sing praises.**

For God is King of all the earth:
B **sing to him a psalm of praise.**

God is seated on his throne:
A **he rules the nations of the world.**

The leaders of the nations come:
B **as subjects of our holy God.**

The lords of earth belong to God:
ALL **he reigns supreme. Amen.**

11.19 PSALM
Psalm 99.1–9†

The congregation may divide at A and B

The Lord reigns:
A **let the nations tremble!**

He sits enthroned on high:
B **let the earth shake!**

Great is the Lord our God:
ALL **exalted over all the world.**

Let the nations praise his awesome name, and say:
A **God is holy!**

Praise the Lord our God, and worship at his feet:
B **God is holy!**

Exalt the Lord our God, and worship on his holy mountain:
ALL **The Lord our God is holy! Amen**

11.22 CREED
From 'TeDeum', Editors

Let us confess our faith in Christ:

**We believe in Christ
the King of glory,
the eternal Son of the Father:
he became man to set us free,
and did not despise the Virgin's womb;
he overcame death,
and opened the kingdom of heaven
    to all believers;
he is seated at God's right hand
    in glory,
and will come to be our judge. Amen.**

11.23 CREED
From Ephesians 2†

Let us declare our faith in the resurrection and reign of Christ:

**By his mighty power,
God raised from the dead
our Lord Jesus Christ
and seated him at his right hand
    in heaven,
far above all rule and authority,
power and dominion,**

**and every title that can be given,
not only in the present age
but also in the age to come.
God placed all things under his feet
and appointed him
to be head over everything
    for the Church,
which is his body,
the fullness of him who fills everything
everywhere and always. Amen.**

11.24 CREED
From Colossians 1†

Let us declare our faith in the supremacy of Christ:

**Christ is the image of the invisible God,
the first-born over all creation.
For by him all things were created:
things in heaven and on earth,
visible and invisible;
thrones, powers, rulers and authorities –
all things were created
    by him and for him.
He is before all things,
and in him all things hold together.**

**He is the head of the body, the Church;
he is the beginning
and the first-born from among the dead,
so that in everything
he might have the supremacy.**

**God was pleased
to have all his fullness dwell in him,
and through him
to reconcile to himself all things;
things on earth and things in heaven,
by making peace through his blood
shed on the cross. Alleluia. Amen.**

11.25 FOR CONFIDENCE IN CHRIST
From Hebrews 4†

O Jesus, Son of God, our high priest
who has gone into the heavens,
you are able to understand
    our weaknesses;
for you have been tempted in every way,
just as we are – yet without sin:
give us confidence

→

that we may approach
   the throne of grace
to receive mercy
and find grace to help us
in our time of need:
to the glory of God the Father. **Amen.**

11.26   FOR STRENGTH
Michael Botting

Lord Jesus Christ,
we thank you that you ascended as king
   of heaven and earth,
and that you are in control of all things:
help us to trust you in joy and in sorrow,
and to obey you always;
for the honour of your name. **Amen.**

11.29   THANKSGIVING
From Revelation 1†

Jesus Christ,
faithful witness, firstborn from the dead,
ruler of the powers of this world:
we thank you that you love us,
and by your sacrificial death
have freed us from our sins
and made us a kingdom of priests
to serve our God and Father:
to you, Lord Jesus
be glory and power for ever and ever!
Amen.

11.30   THANKSGIVING
Editors

O Lord our God, we thank you for the
privilege of living in a world filled with
variety and beauty, and for the challenge
of its mysteries.

For the gift of loving and being loved, for
friendship and mutual understanding: O
Lord, we give you thanks,
and lift up our hearts in praise.

For the richness of our world; for forests
and fields, for mountains and oceans: O
God, we give you thanks,
and lift up our hearts in praise.

For the delights of music and poetry,
for other people's thoughts and
conversations, and for all good books
and reading: O God, we give you thanks,
and lift up our hearts in praise.

For the refreshing power of the falling
rain, for the strength and vitality of the
shining sun, and for every life-giving
source: O God, we give you thanks,
and lift up our hearts in praise.

Above all we thank you
for the grace of your Spirit
flowing into our lives
and recreating them
in the image of Jesus our redeemer.
Amen.

11.31   ACCLAMATION
Unknown, adapted

We praise our ascended and exalted
Lord:

Name above every name: Jesus, Lord,
we worship and adore you.

King of righteousness, king of peace,
enthroned at the right hand of Majesty on
high: Jesus, Lord,
we worship and adore you.

Send us out in his power
to live and work
   to your praise and glory;
through him to whom we belong,
Jesus Christ our Lord. Amen.

11.32   ASCRIPTION
From Revelation 4 and 5†

Let us give glory to God:

Our Lord and God, you are worthy to
receive glory, honour, and power; for
you created all things, and by your will
they were given existence and life:
Glory to God in the highest!

O Lamb of God, you are worthy to
receive wisdom, strength, and praise, for
by your death you bought for God

people from every tribe, language, nation and race:
Glory to God in the highest!

You have made them a kingdom of priests to serve our God, and they shall rule on earth:
Glory to God in the highest!

**To him who sits upon the throne
and to the Lamb,
be praise and honour,
glory and power,
for ever and ever! Amen.**

11.33   ADORATION
Editors

Lord Jesus Christ,
thank you for your unfailing mercy
and infinite love:
through our sweet communion with you
we have seen the Father.

Lord, King of heaven and earth,
we worship and adore you,
today, tomorrow and for ever. **Amen.**

The Holy Spirit

12.1   GREETING
From 2 Timothy 4†

The Lord be with your spirit:
grace and peace be with you. Amen.

12.8   RESPONSE
From Acts 2 and Romans 5†

'In the last days,' God says, 'I will pour out my Spirit on all people':
**God's love
has been poured out into our hearts
by the Holy Spirit
whom he has given us. Amen.**

12.9   RESPONSE
From Galatians 5†

The fruit of the Spirit is love, joy, peace, patience, kindness, goodness, faithfulness, gentleness and self-control:
**since we live by the Spirit,
let us walk in the Spirit. Amen.**

12.10   APPROACH
Editors

With joy and gladness we celebrate your power and presence, Holy Spirit of God. By your energy the world was formed and made, darkness gave place to light, men and women were fashioned and became living beings, able to know God, to hear God speaking, and to respond to God calling. Through you, Holy Spirit, the word of God has come to us through prophets and preachers; by your inspiration poets and musicians have composed works of praise; by your operation, faith and hope in Jesus Christ has been born in us, your Church has sprung to life, your gifts and graces have been distributed, new life and wholeness has come to Christ's body:

**To you, Holy Spirit –
giving eternal life,
glorifying Jesus,
exalting God our heavenly Father –
be glory now and for evermore. Amen.**

12.11   PRAISE
From Psalm 103†

Praise the Lord, O my soul,
all my being, praise his name!

Praise the Lord, O my soul,
and do not forget his blessings!

Praise the Lord, O my soul.
Praise the Lord. Amen.

12.12 CONFESSION
Editors

Almighty God,
we confess that we have sinned
  against you:
for we have denied
  your saving presence in our lives,
and we have grieved your Holy Spirit.
Come to us in the fire of your love,
and set our minds
  on the things of the Spirit,
that we may share his gifts
  and bear his fruit
in love and joy and peace;
through Jesus Christ our Lord. Amen.

12.16 PSALM
Psalm 51.6–12 and Psalm 143.6–10†

O Lord, I spread my hands out to you:
I thirst for you like dry ground.

Teach me to do your will, for you are my God:
let your good Spirit lead me in safety.

You require sincerity and truth in me:
fill my mind with your wisdom.

Create in me a pure heart, O God:
renew a faithful spirit in me.

Do not cast me from your presence:
or take your Holy Spirit from me.

Give me again the joy of your salvation:
and make me willing to obey. Amen.

12.17 PSALM
Psalm 104.1–4, 29–30†

O Lord our God, you are very great:
you are clothed with splendour
  and majesty.

You make winds your messengers:
and flashes of fire your servants.

How many are your works:
the earth is full of your creatures!

When you hide your face, they are afraid:
when you take away their breath,
they die.

When you send your Spirit they are created:
and you renew the face of the earth.
Amen.

12.19 CREED
From Revelation 1†

Let us declare our faith in God:

We believe in God the Father;
the almighty,
who was, and is, and is to come.

We believe in Jesus Christ;
the faithful witness,
the firstborn from the dead,
the King of kings,
who loves us,
and has freed us from our sins
  by his blood.

We believe in the Spirit;
giver of many gifts,
proceeding from the throne on high.

We believe in one God:
Father, Son, and Holy Spirit. Amen.

12.20 FOR THE HOLY SPIRIT
Editors

O, Holy Spirit of God,
come to us and cleanse us, we pray:
fill us with your love and truth
  and wisdom,
and make us your temples
  of holiness and peace;
grant us your precious gift of faith,
so that bonded with Christ
we may know the joy of serving him.
Spirit divine,
draw us into your pure light;
bless us and possess us,
for the sake of our Saviour, Jesus Christ.
Amen.

12.23 FOR THE SPIRIT'S POWER
Editors

O Lord God, fill us, we pray, with the power of your Holy Spirit:

Grant us your peace, that we may stand firm and remain quiet in trouble. Lord,
grant us your peace.

Grant us your courage, that we may speak of you and of your love when the time is ripe. Lord,
grant us your courage.

Grant us your calmness to think clearly and wisely in the face of crisis or pressure. Lord,
grant us your calmness.

Grant us your confidence to know that in all things you are finally in charge and that nothing can separate us from your love. Lord,
grant us your confidence.

Grant us your obedience to accept what has to be in our lives and to put aside resentment, bitterness and envy which destroys. Lord,
grant us your obedience.

O God,
pour out upon us all these graces
   of your Holy Spirit
that we may hold firm to our faith,
and to our life's end be good witnesses
to our Lord Jesus Christ. Amen.

12.24 FOR GOD'S SPIRIT
Based on Galatians 5

We pray that God's Holy Spirit may direct our lives:

'The fruit of the Spirit is love, joy and peace' – Father, we know that our world needs love and harmony: come to bless us,
and fill us with your Spirit.

'The fruit of the Spirit is patience, kindness and goodness' – Father, we know that our world is starved of compassion and true fellowship: come to bless us,
and fill us with your Spirit.

'The fruit of the Spirit is faithfulness, gentleness and self-control'—Father, we know that our world is short of truth and justice: come to bless us,
and fill us with your Spirit.

Send us out in his power
to live and work
   to your praise and glory;
through him to whom we belong,
Jesus Christ our Lord. Amen.

12.26   THANKSGIVING
            FOR THE SPIRIT
Editors

'The Spirit of God was hovering over the waters.' For your Spirit's power in creation, bringing life and light to birth; for his creative power in us today, O God, we thank you:
from our hearts we thank you.

'The Spirit of God came upon them.' That your Spirit energised the prophets to speak your word, and guided the leaders of your people; that he speaks and leads today, O God, we thank you:
from our hearts we thank you.

'The Spirit descended on him like a dove.' That your Spirit identified your Son Jesus, and filled him for ministry; that he reveals him to us and leads us into all truth, O God, we thank you:
from our hearts we thank you.

'All of them were filled with the Holy Spirit.' That on the day of Pentecost the Spirit came to your waiting disciples, enriching them with your gifts and driving them out to work and witness for you; that he renews and empowers your Church today, equipping us for service by many gifts, O God, we thank you:
from our hearts we thank you.

'The Spirit of God is living in us.' That your Spirit is in each of us, giving life to our mortal bodies, putting to death our sinful nature, proving to us that we are God's children and heirs of his grace,

→

helping us in our weakness, interceding
for us in prayers beyond words, O God,
we thank you:
from our hearts we thank you.

**Spirit of God, Spirit of Jesus,
creator Spirit, life-giving Spirit,
encouraging Spirit, cleansing Spirit,
healing Spirit, gracious Spirit,
O holy Spirit, come! Amen.**

12.27   THANKSGIVING
Editors

We rejoice, our God, in the multitude of
gifts you have given. For music, in all its
variety and harmony, which expresses
our deep feelings and desires, thank you:
to you be the glory, O Lord.

For art in all its forms, portraying nature,
expressing inward beauty, evoking our
response, satisfying our emotions, thank
you:
to you be the glory, O Lord.

For your life-creating and sustaining
Spirit, in these last days poured out upon
us your family to energise our service
and to lead us into all truth, thank you:
to you be the glory, O Lord.

**Receive our thanks for all your gifts,
and let them be used
for the glory of your name. Amen.**

12.28   THANKSGIVING
Editors

O God, we are your people, you are our
creator; your loving kindness is without
end; your faithfulness abounds.
Almighty God:
we praise you and adore you.

We can never praise you enough for the
presence of the Lord Jesus in this world:
the majesty of your being is displayed in
him; the way into your presence we find
through him. Almighty God:
we praise you and adore you.

You flow into our lives by the Holy Spirit
whose coming brings us joy and peace.

Our weakness and shallowness is
transformed by his strength, our darkest
moments enlightened by his presence.
Almighty God:
we praise you and adore you.

**To you, our God, be praise
now and for ever,
Father, Son and Holy Spirit. Amen.**

12.29   THANKSGIVING
Christopher Idle

We thank you, God our Father,
for sending your Holy Spirit
to guide and strengthen us,
to help us understand the Bible,
and to love and serve the Lord Jesus;
for his sake. **Amen.**

12.31   FOR HOLINESS:
A PERSONAL PRAYER
Editors

Breathe on me, Holy Spirit;
cleanse and sanctify me,
so that I may offer
    all my praise,
    all my service,
    all my devotion,
    all my love,
through Jesus the Son
to God the Father. **Amen.**

12.32   DEDICATION:
A PERSONAL PRAYER
Editors

Ever-gracious Holy Spirit:
come to me in your perfect power,
and take possession of my life;
help me to understand more about Jesus
    and his sacrifice on the Cross,
and help me to live out my gratitude.
Draw me ever nearer to my Lord
    and Saviour,
and never let me stray from his side.
Spirit of God,
receive me as I receive you,
in Jesus' name. **Amen.**

13.1 GREETING
From 2 Thessalonians†

Grace and peace to you from God our Father and the Lord Jesus Christ. **Amen.**

13.8 RESPONSE
From Romans 11†

Oh, the depth of the riches of the wisdom and knowledge of God!
How unsearchable his judgements, and his paths beyond tracing out!

13.9 RESPONSE
From Isaiah 6†

Holy, holy, holy is the Lord almighty:
the whole earth is full of his glory. Amen.

13.10 RESPONSE
From Psalm 104†

O Lord our God, you are very great:
**you are clothed with splendour
    and majesty.**

Praise the Lord, O my soul:
Praise the Lord. Amen.

13.13 APPROACH
Editors

**Great and mighty is our Lord God,
his wisdom cannot be measured.
He takes pleasure
    in those who honour him,
in those who trust in his constant love.**

Lord God, our loving Father in heaven, creator of this magnificent world – all your works praise you in all places of your dominion. Lord, you are great and mighty:
your wisdom cannot be measured.

We rejoice this day in your goodness, we are amazed at every indication of your interest in us. You are the Lord of the universe, the King of kings, yet you care for all your creatures. You are the Lord of lords and yet you reach down in loving compassion and tender mercy even to the most contemptible of human sinners. Lord, you are great and mighty:
your wisdom cannot be measured.

You have inexhaustible desires to bless your people; yours is a mercy that knows no bounds, a love which penetrates all barriers, a forgiveness which reaches to all our guiltiness. Lord, you are great and mighty:
your wisdom cannot be measured.

We gladly and fervently offer you our worship and praise. We join the whole creation in heaven and on earth to acknowledge your sovereignty, and we rest wholly in your salvation revealed in Jesus Christ our Lord. **Amen.**

13.14 APPROACH
Editors

This is the day that the Lord has made:
let us rejoice and be glad in it.

O give thanks to the Lord for he is good:
his steadfast love endures for ever.

13.15 PRAISE
From Revelation 19†

Praise our God, all you his servants, you who fear him, both small and great:
**Alleluia!
For our Lord God almighty reigns.**

Let us rejoice and be glad and give him the glory:
Amen.

13.16   PRAISE
From Psalm 104†

Praise the Lord, O my soul;
praise the Lord!

O Lord my God, how great you are;
robed in majesty and splendour.

Praise the Lord, O my soul;
praise the Lord! Amen.

13.17   CONFESSION
From Isaiah 6†

**O Lord our God,
enthroned on high,
filling the whole earth with your glory:
holy, holy, holy is your name.
Our eyes have seen the King,
the Lord almighty;
but our lips are unclean.
We cry to you in our sinfulness
to take our guilt away,
through Jesus Christ our Lord. Amen.**

13.18   CONFESSION
From Isaiah 57†

**O God,
you are eternal, and your name is holy;
you live in a high and holy place –
yet also with the humble and penitent:
revive our spirits,
renew our hearts;
do not accuse us, nor be angry for ever.
We confess our greed
and our wilful ways:
you have punished us
and you have hidden your face
    from us:
O God, forgive us,
through Jesus Christ our Lord. Amen.**

13.19   CONFESSION
Editors

Others may help the minister in leading this prayer at A, B and C

We confess to you, our Father, our small-mindedness and limited appreciation of your greatness and almighty power.

A   We confess that we scarcely consider your mighty movements at the beginning of time, creating the heavens and the earth. Lord, we have sinned:
**forgive us,
    and enlarge our understanding.**

We confess that the life and death and resurrection of our Lord Jesus Christ do not infuse our thinking as they should; we are so hemmed in by transitory interests and temporal pursuits that we lose sight of the essential and eternal issues. Lord, we have sinned:
forgive us, and deepen our love.

c   We confess that we do not value, and often do not welcome, the gift of your Holy Spirit to liberate our tongues to praise you and our lives to serve you. Lord, we have sinned:
forgive us, and set us free.

**Father, forgive us for our failures
    and our sins,
through the love of our Lord Jesus;
and help us by the power
    of your Holy Spirit. Amen.**

13.21   COLLECT
Trinity Sunday, ASB 1980

Almighty and eternal God,
you have revealed yourself
as Father, Son, and Holy Spirit,
and live and reign
in the perfect unity of love.
Hold us firm in this faith,
that we may know you in all your ways
and evermore rejoice
    in your eternal glory,
who are three Persons in one God,
now and for ever. **Amen.**

13.22   PSALM
Psalm 8.1–9†

The congregation may divide at A, B and C

O Lord, our Lord:
**how great is your name
    in all the world!**

A **Your glory fills the skies.**
B **Your praise is sung by children.**
C **You silence your enemies.**

I look at the sky your hands have made, the moon and stars you put in place:
ALL **Who are we that you care for us?**

You made us less than gods:
ALL **to crown us with glory and honour.**

You put us in charge of creation:
A **the beasts of the field.**
B **the birds of the air.**
C **the fish of the sea.**

O Lord, our Lord:
ALL **how great is your name
in all the world! Amen.**

13.23 PSALM
Psalm 97.1–12†

The congregation may divide at A, B and C

The Lord is king:
the Lord is king!

Let the whole wide earth rejoice:
A **let the islands all be glad.**

Thunder-clouds encircle him:
B **truth and justice are his throne.**

Fire shall go before the Lord:
C **burning up his enemies.**

Lightning strikes the darkened world:
A **all the people see and fear.**

Mountains melt before our God:
B **he is Lord of all the earth.**

Skies proclaim his righteousness:
C **nations see his glory now.**

Idol-worshippers are shamed:
A **gods bow down before the Lord.**

Let Jerusalem rejoice:
B **in your faithful judgements, Lord!**

Sovereign of the universe:
C **mightier still than all the gods!**

Yet you help your saints, O Lord:
A **saving them from wicked men.**

Light will shine upon the good:
B **gladness fill the righteous heart.**

Now recall what God has done:
C **thank him,**
B **praise him,**
ALL **and rejoice! Amen.**

13.25 CREED
From Psalm 145†

**We believe in God
who is gracious and compassionate,
slow to anger and rich in love.**

**We believe in God,
whose kingdom is everlasting,
whose dominion endures for ever.**

**We believe in God,
who is faithful to all his promises,
and loving towards all he has made.**

**We believe in God,
who opens his hand
and satisfies the needs
of all things living. Amen.**

13.26 CREED
From 'The Athanasian Creed', Editors

Let us declare the universal Christian Faith:

**We worship one God in trinity,
and trinity in unity;
neither confusing the persons
nor dividing the nature of God.
For there is one person of the Father,
another of the Son,
and another of the Holy Spirit;
but the Godhead of the Father,
of the Son, and of the Holy Spirit
is all one –
the glory equal,
the majesty co-eternal:
what the Father is, so is the Son
and so is the Holy Spirit. Amen.**

13.27   FOR HOLINESS
From 'Contemporay Parish Prayers', adapted

Father, Son and Holy Spirit,
Lord of majesty,
Trinity of love and power:
accept and make holy
    all that we are,
    all that we have,
    and all that we offer you.
Keep us firm in our faith
and strong in your service;
create in us a new heart,
that we may respond
    to your great mercy:
one God, our saviour,
now and for ever. **Amen.**

13.29   THANKSGIVING
Editors

Three persons A, B and C may lead this prayer

A Father Almighty, for your majesty and your mercy – loving us still in our waywardness, forgiving us in our unworthiness: we bring you our worship **and offer you thanksgiving.**

B Jesus, our Redeemer, for your humility and your sacrifice – sharing our joys and sorrows, dying and rising for our salvation: we bring you our worship **and offer you thanksgiving.**

C Holy Spirit of God, for your guidance and your encouragement – inspiring and empowering the church, revealing to us all truth: we bring you our worship **and offer you thanksgiving.**

God of gods –
Father, Son and Holy Spirit,
eternal Lord, Three-in-One:
to you be glory, honour and praise,
for ever and ever. Amen.

13.30   THANKSGIVING
Editors

Two persons A and B, may lead this prayer

A We praise and adore you, our heavenly Father, that in your grace and providence you richly fill our lives.

B You created the world, commanding light to shine out of darkness, making us in your moral image; and you have shone into our minds and hearts, bringing wisdom and power.

A&B Father, we thank you:
ALL **we worship and adore you.**

A We praise and adore you, Lord Jesus Christ, who on the first day of the week rose from the dead in triumph.

B You brought immortality to light; you have shown us the dawn beyond the darkness. Your word and your power have brought to us the Kingdom of God.

A&B Jesus, we thank you:
ALL **we worship and adore you.**

A We praise and adore you, Holy Spirit, for you revealed your power on the day of Pentecost; and today you are at work in our lives, filling us with the love of the Father, giving us understanding and wisdom.

B You illumine the Scriptures, bringing understanding to our darkened minds; you share your gifts among us to build your church into a spiritual household; you confirm your presence within our lives, giving us love for one another.

A&B Holy Spirit, we thank you:
ALL **we worship and adore you.**

ALL **God almighty,**
    Father, Son and Holy Spirit,
    to you be praise for ever and ever.
    Amen.

13.31 THANKSGIVING
Editors

Father, we thank you:
we worship and adore you.

Jesus, we thank you:
we worship and adore you.

Holy Spirit, we thank you:
we worship and adore you.

O God almighty,
Father, Son and Holy Spirit,
to you be praise for ever and ever.
Amen.

13.32 ASCRIPTION
From Revelation 15†

Great and marvellous are your deeds,
　　Lord God almighty;
just and true are your ways,
　　King of the ages.
Who will not fear you, O Lord,
and bring glory to your name?
For you alone are holy;
all nations will come
　　and worship before you,
for your righteous acts
　　have been revealed. **Amen.**

13.34 ASCRIPTION
From Revelation 15†

Glory be to you, O God,
Father, Son, and Holy Spirit,
you have power, wisdom and majesty:
receive from us
honour, glory, worship and blessing.
Great and marvellous are your works,
just and true are your ways:
blessing and honour
　　and glory and power
be to him who reigns upon the throne,
and to the Lamb,
through the one eternal Spirit,
now and for ever. **Amen.**

13.36 DOXOLOGY
From Romans 11†

O Lord our God, how profound are the
riches of your wisdom and knowledge;
how unsearchable your judgements, and
your paths beyond tracing out!
Who has known your mind, O Lord;
who has been your counsellor?
Who has ever given to you,
that you should repay?

For from you and through you and to
you are all things:
yours be the glory for ever! Amen.

13.37 DOXOLOGY
Alan Gaunt

You are the one and only God; there is
none like you, Lord; you are great and
your name is holy:
glorify your name.

By the worship of your Church in every
generation, by our worship today:
glorify your name.

By the proclamation of the coming of
Jesus, by his reception in our hearts:
glorify your name.

By the winning of the world and the
reconciliation of all people:
glorify your name.

By the living of our lives in faith, by the
labour of our love and by our hope in the
Lord Jesus Christ:
glorify your name.

Our Lord God,
you have glorified it,
and you will glorify it again:
glorify your name in us. Amen.

13.38 DOXOLOGY
From 'A New Zealand Prayer Book'

Great is the Lord and worthy of all
praise:
Amen!
Praise and glory and wisdom,
thanksgiving and honour,
   power and might,
be to our God for ever and ever! Amen.

Sea Theme, Holidays

14.1   GREETING
From Titus 1†

Grace and peace from God the Father
and Christ Jesus our Saviour. **Amen.**

14.7   RESPONSE
From Psalm 24†

The earth is the Lord's
   and everything in it:
the world and all who live here.

14.8   RESPONSE
From Psalm 104†

There is the sea, vast and spacious,
teeming with creatures beyond number –
living things both large and small:
how many are your works, O Lord!
in wisdom you have made them all.

14.9   RESPONSE
From Mark 4†

Jesus rebuked the wind and said to the
waves: 'Be quiet!' The disciples said:
Who is this?
Even the wind and the waves obey him!

14.10   RESPONSE
From Psalm 107†

Those who went out to the sea in ships,
merchants on the mighty waters, were
glad when the Lord guided them to their
desired haven:
Let them give thanks to the Lord
for his unfailing love. Amen.

14.12   APPROACH
Unknown, adapted Editors

Three persons A, B and C may assist with
leading this prayer

We have come to worship God our
Father; to acknowledge his power and
authority, to give thanks for his care and
keeping, and to offer ourselves in the
service of Christ:

A He is Creator of the world:
   he gives us life and breath.

B He is Preserver of all life:
   he sustains us day by day.

C He is Redeemer of his people:
   he shows us his love in Christ.

A, B and C He is Lord of lords:
   he controls all things.

O God our Father,
we bring you our love and praise
and give you thanks
   for all your goodness,
through Jesus Christ our Lord. Amen.

14.14   PRAISE
From Psalm 98†

Sing to the Lord a new song,
for he has done marvellous things!

Sing for joy to the Lord, all the earth;
praise him
with songs and shouts of joy! Amen.

14.15   CONFESSION
C S Woodward, adapted

O God, our gracious Father,
we confess that we have sinned
against you
and done many things to grieve you:
we have often been selfish,
we have sometimes forgotten
to pray to you,
and we have not loved you
as we should.
For these and all other sins
forgive us, we pray,
through him who died for us,
Jesus Christ our Lord. Amen.

14.16   CONFESSION
Editors

Creator God, we confess that we fail to
value your creation. We take so much for
granted without thanking you, the giver
of every good thing; we exploit the
world, we abuse its resources; we pollute
the earth, the sky, the sea. O God, forgive
us:
have mercy on us.

We confess that we fail to heed the
Bible's teaching about the earth – that it
is the good work of your hands, given
into our care, waiting for redemption.
And we forget that we shall be called to
account for our stewardship. O God,
forgive us:
have mercy on us.

We confess that we think too little of the
new creation in our Lord Jesus Christ.
We are slow to follow him, we do not

firmly trust in his forgiveness, we do not
fully share in his resurrection life. O God,
forgive us:
have mercy on us.

Help us in your mercy
to receive your forgiveness,
and strengthen us to serve you well;
for the sake of Jesus Christ our Lord.
Amen.

14.17   CONFESSION
From Psalm 130†

Out of the depths, O Lord, we cry to you.
O Lord, hear our voice:
listen to our cry for mercy.

If you kept a record of our sins, who
could stand before you? O Lord, hear our
voice:
listen to our cry for mercy.

But you offer forgiveness, and therefore
we fear you. O Lord, hear our voice:
listen to our cry for mercy.

We wait for you, O Lord, and in your
promise we put our hope. O Lord, hear
our voice:
listen to our cry for mercy.

We long for you, O Lord, more than the
sleepless long for the morning. O Lord,
hear our voice:
listen to our cry for mercy.

O God, we put our trust in you,
because with you there is unfailing love
and full redemption from all our sins;
through our Saviour Jesus Christ.
Amen.

14.19   COLLECT
From 'The Scottish Prayer Book', adapted

Almighty God,
you led your people through the sea,
and made a path for them
in deep waters:
be near all those
who face the dangers of the seas;
protect them from disaster,

→

help them on their way,
and bring them safely
  to their desired haven
with hearts thankful for your mercy;
through Jesus Christ our Lord. **Amen.**

14.20 PSALM
Psalm 93. 1–5†

The congregation may divide at A and B

The Lord reigns, robed in majesty:
A **he arms himself with power.**

The earth is firmly set in place:
B **it never can be moved.**

Your throne was founded long ago:
A **before all time began.**

The oceans raise their voice, O Lord:
B **and lift their roaring waves.**

The Lord is mightier than the sea:
A **he rules supreme on high.**

His laws stand firm through endless
days:
B **his praise for evermore.**
ALL **Amen.**

14.21 PSALM
Psalm 107. 1–31†

The congregation may divide at A and B.

Give thanks to the Lord, for he is
good:
his love endures for ever.

Repeat these words in praise to the
Lord:
all those he has redeemed.

Some sailed the ocean in ships:
A **they earned their way on the seas.**

They saw what the Lord can do:
B **his wonderful deeds in the deep.**

For he spoke and stirred up a storm:
A **and lifted high the waves.**

Their ships were thrown in the air:
B **and plunged into the depths.**

Their courage melted away:
A **they reeled like drunken men.**

They came to the end of themselves:
B **and cried to the Lord**
   in their trouble.

He brought them out of distress:
A **and stilled the raging storm.**

They were glad because of the calm:
B **he brought them safely to harbour.**

Let them give thanks to the Lord:
ALL **for his unfailing love. Amen**

14.23 CREED
From 'Te Deum', Editors

Let us acclaim the Lord our God:

We believe in God
the eternal Father;
heaven and earth are full of his glory.

We believe in Jesus Christ,
his true and only Son;
he became man to set us free.

We believe in the Holy Spirit;
he is our advocate and guide.

We believe in one God:
Father, Son, and Holy Spirit. Amen.

14.30 FOR TRAVELLERS
From 'New Every Morning'

O God, our Father,
we commend to your keeping
those who travel by land or sea or air:
give them your protection on their way,
and bring them safely
   to their journey's end;
through Jesus Christ our Lord. **Amen.**

14.34 THANKSGIVING
Editors

We thank God for the wonderful world
he has given to us, and for all his love
and care:

For the warmth of the sun, O God of
love,
we give you thanks and praise.

For the rain which makes things grow, O God of love,
we give you thanks and praise.

For the woods and the fields, O God of love,
we give you thanks and praise.

For the sea and the sky, O God of love,
we give you thanks and praise.

For the flowers and the animals, O God of love,
we give you thanks and praise.

For families and holidays, O God of love,
we give you thanks and praise.

For all your gifts, O God of love,
we give you thanks and praise.

Everything around us rejoices:
therefore give us joyful hearts
to praise you in your glory;
through Jesus Christ our Lord. Amen.

14.35 DOXOLOGY
From Romans 11†

O Lord our God
how profound are the riches
of your wisdom and knowledge;

how unsearchable your judgments,
and your paths beyond tracing out!
Who has known your mind, O Lord;
who has been your counsellor?
Who has ever given to you,
that you should repay?

For from you and through you and to you are all things:
yours be the glory for ever! Amen.

14.36 ASCRIPTION
From 1 Chronicles 29†

Lord God, may you be praised for ever and ever:

You are great and powerful,
glorious, splendid and majestic;
everything in heaven and earth is yours
and you are king,
supreme ruler over all;
all riches and wealth come from you;
you rule everything
by your strength and power;
you alone are able
   to make anyone great and strong:
now, our God, we give you thanks
and praise your glorious name. Amen.

God's Love to Us, Our Response

15.1 GREETING
From Jude†

You are loved by God the Father and kept by Jesus Christ:
mercy, peace and love
   be ours for ever. Amen.

15.7 RESPONSE
From Psalm 103†

The steadfast love of the Lord is from everlasting to everlasting upon those who fear him:
his righteousness
to our children's children. Amen.

15.8 RESPONSE
From Psalm 145†

The Lord is gracious and merciful:
his compassion
is over all that he has made.

15.9 RESPONSE
From 1 John 4†

Dear friends, since God so loved us, we ought also to love one another:
if we love one another,
God lives in us,
and his love is made perfect in us.
Amen.

15.10 RESPONSE
From 1 John 4†

God loved us:
**and sent his Son
to be the means by which
    our sins are forgiven.**

15.14 PRAISE
From Psalm 92†

It is good to praise you, Lord,
and make music to your name:

To proclaim your constant love in the morning,
and tell your faithfulness in the evening.

For you, O Lord, are exalted for ever.
Amen.

15.15 PRAISE
From Psalm 106†

Give thanks to the Lord, for he is good;
his love endures for ever.

Tell of all his mighty acts;
and make his praises heard.

Praise be to the Lord, the God of Israel:
from everlasting to everlasting.

Let all the people say, 'Amen':
Amen, praise the Lord!

15.16 CONFESSION
Editors

Almighty God, we confess that too often we have taken the easy way of the world, rather than your way, and so have grieved your heart of love.

We have been slow to admit that we are not our own, but belong to you: in your mercy,
forgive us and help us.

We have been unwilling to see that we are bought with the price of Christ's blood: in your mercy,
forgive us and help us.

We have been unprepared to live out our lives as your servants: in your mercy,
forgive us and help us.

**Raise us by the power of your love,
and fill us
    with the joy of your Spirit;
through Jesus Christ our Lord. Amen.**

15.17 CONFESSION
Editors

Lord Jesus, as we confess our sins, help us to trust completely in your forgiveness:

For our lack of self-discipline that so often chooses what we wish rather than what we ought to do, in your mercy:
forgive us, dear Lord.

For our half-hearted obedience to your truth and to your way of life for your disciples, in your mercy:
forgive us, dear Lord.

For our failure to serve others, and for our neglect of those who are defeated by their poverty, their loneliness or their lack of opportunity, in your mercy:
forgive us, dear Lord.

For our sin and foolishness which has made it easier for others to neglect your truth and to doubt your everlasting love, in your mercy:
forgive us, dear Lord.

**By your grace forgive us;
by your strength
    help us to amend our ways
and glorify you for ever. Amen.**

15.18 CONFESSION
From Psalm 130†

**O Lord, we cry to you
    from the depths of our being:
let your ears be open
    as we plead for mercy.
If you kept a record of our sins
none of us could stand before you;
but you alone can forgive us,
therefore we come to you in awe.**

Lord, we wait for you
and in your promise we put our hope;
through our saviour Jesus Christ. Amen.

15.20 COLLECT
Pentecost 16, ASB 1980

Almighty God,
you have taught us through your Son
that love is the fulfilling of the law.
Grant that we may love you
  with our whole heart
and our neighbours as ourselves;
through Jesus Christ our Lord. **Amen.**

15.21 COLLECT
From 'Morning Prayer', ASB 1980

Eternal God and Father,
you create us by your power
and redeem us by your love:
guide and strengthen us
  by your Spirit,
that we may give ourselves
  in love and service
to one another and to you;
through Jesus Christ our Lord. **Amen.**

15.22 PSALM
Psalm 36.5–9†

The congregation – and ministers – may
divide at A and B

Your love, O Lord, reaches the
heavens:
A **your faithfulness**
  extends to the skies.

Your righteousness is towering like
the mountains:
B **your justice is like the great deep.**

How precious is your love, O God:
A **we find shelter**
  beneath your wings!

We feast on the food you provide:
B **we drink**
  from the river of your goodness.

For with you is the fountain of
life:
ALL **in your light we see light. Amen.**

15.24 CREED
From John 1†

We believe in God the Father,
who reveals his love to us in Christ.

We believe in God the Son,
who pours out his Holy Spirit on us.

We believe in the Holy Spirit,
who teaches us God's truth.

We believe in one God:
Father, Son, and Holy Spirit. Amen.

15.25 ADORATION
Editors

Lord God of earth and heaven, we praise
you because you are the source of all life,
all joy and all true love.

For your mighty power, creating the
universe, stretching out the heavens,
controlling the planets in their orbit, Lord
God of earth and heaven,
we worship and adore you.

For your incessant searching and caring
for us, though we are a selfish, rebellious
and sinful people, Lord God of earth and
heaven,
we worship and adore you.

For your love revealed in Jesus Christ,
which assaults the stubbornness of our
unbelief; for the grace and truth which
have come to us in him, and for our
redemption, Lord God of earth and
heaven,
we worship and adore you.

O Lord God eternal,
greater in majesty than we can imagine,
stronger than any power
  which we can comprehend,
closer to us than we can ever believe,
more aware of our needs
  than we can express in words;
Father, Son and Holy Spirit,
we worship and adore you
for ever and ever. Amen.

**15.32 FOR CONTENTMENT
IN CHRIST**
Simon Baynes

O God, make us more thankful
for what we have received,
more content with what we have,
and more mindful
   of other people in need:
we ask it for his sake
who lived for us in poverty,
Jesus Christ our Lord. **Amen.**

15.33 THANKSGIVING
Editors

Heavenly Father, we thank you
for the beauty of the world around us;
for the love of parents and friends,
for work and play,
   for food and clothes,
for happiness, laughter and fun.
But most of all we thank you
   for your redeeming grace:
for the birth of Jesus Christ your Son,
for the example of his life,
and the love
   which made him die for us.
Help us to serve him faithfully
   all our days. **Amen.**

**15.34 THANKSGIVING
FOR ALL GOD'S GIFTS**
Editors

O heavenly Father,
we thank you for the good things
   you so richly provide;
we thank you for your wisdom
given when we ask you;
and we thank you for your love for us,
unasked and underserved.
Give us ever thankful hearts,
and always a sense of how much
   we owe you,
then help us
to serve you as you deserve;
through Jesus Christ our Lord. **Amen.**

15.35 THANKFULNESS
Editors

'Bless the Lord, my soul, and do not
forget all his blessings!' Each day we
thank you, Lord:
and praise your name for ever.

For every ray of light you send into our
darkened minds that we may recall our
blessings, we thank you, Lord:
and praise your name for ever.

For every glimpse of beauty we have
seen in this world, we thank you, Lord:
and praise your name for ever.

For every sign of your perfection and
creative will, we thank you, Lord:
and praise your name for ever.

For every echo of your truth amid the
world's deceit and hypocrisy, we thank
you, Lord:
and praise your name for ever.

For every reflection of your love we have
seen in family and friends, we thank you,
Lord:
and praise your name for ever.

For every opportunity to serve you –
even in small tasks and unrewarding
duties – we thank you, Lord:
and praise your name for ever.

That you gave your Son to be our
Saviour, and that with him you have
freely given us all things, we thank you,
Lord:
and praise your name for ever.

**Lord,
help us always to recall your blessings,
and to praise your name for ever. Amen.**

15.36 THANKSGIVING
Editors

We praise you, heavenly Father, for the
wonder of your love:

For the generous scale of creation, for the
abundance of earth's resources, and for
the number and variety of peoples you
have made, we give you thanks today,
and praise you for your love.

That in your love you did not spare your only Son but freely gave him up to come as our Saviour into the world; that in love he lived among us, and for us sinners died on the cross to effect our redemption; that he rose again on the third day to lead us to heaven, we give you thanks today,
and praise you for your love.

For your grace of forgiveness which covers our sin, for the variety of gifts of the Spirit given to your Church, and for sharing our pain, our sickness and our dying, we give you thanks today,
and praise you for your love.

For these and all your other
gifts of providence and grace,
we thank you
in the name of the Lord Jesus Christ.
Amen.

15.37 THANKSGIVING
FOR JESUS' FRIENDSHIP
Editors

Lord Jesus,
thank you for being our friend:
when we are weak, you strengthen us,
when we are lonely you speak to us,
when we are sad you comfort us,
when we are glad you rejoice with us;
you are our guide, our keeper,
our shepherd, our shield;
your presence is our constant joy,
our prayers are in your name. **Amen.**

OR, AS A PERSONAL PRAYER

Lord Jesus,
thank you for being my friend:
when I am weak, you strengthen me,
when I am lonely you speak to me,
when I am sad you comfort me,
when I am glad you rejoice with me;
you are my guide, my keeper,
my shepherd, my shield;
your presence is my constant joy,
my prayer is in your name. **Amen.**

15.38 THANKSGIVING
FOR HUMAN LIFE
Editors

It is with a sense of deep gratitude, our Eternal God, that we bow head and heart in your presence; in creating us and bringing us to this moment are seen your measureless power and your limitless love:

For all your good gifts given freely to us, we praise you:
O Lord, we bless you,
we thank and praise you!

For our minds, for the gift of thought that enables us to probe mysteries, and in some measure understand some of the wonderful things you have provided for us, we praise you:
O Lord, we bless you,
we thank and praise you!

For the energy of youth, for its infectious quest after life; for visions and for dreams, we praise you:
O Lord, we bless you,
we thank and praise you!

For the experience and maturity of judgement given to older people, whose lives have been moulded by your Holy Spirit, we praise you:
O Lord, we bless you,
we thank and praise you!

For the gift of health – of body, mind and spirit, and for the harmony within us by which a thousand factors work together to produce freedom from pain and from distress of mind, we praise you:
O Lord, we bless you,
we thank and praise you!

Accept our gratitude
for all your blessings
and the response of our love
and service;
through Jesus our Lord. Amen.

15.39   DEDICATION
Editors

O God, we are your children
and you love us:
so deep is your love
that nothing we have done,
   or thought to do,
shall take away the peace you give;
so strong is your love
that no passing trouble
shall tear us from your arms;
so precious is your love

that all our life
shall be lived in your service –
and yours shall be the glory,
through Jesus Christ our Lord. **Amen.**

15.42   BLESSING
From a Scottish folk blessing

The Father's love enfold us,
the grace of Christ uphold us,
the Holy Spirit guide us;
one God to walk beside us. **Amen.**

Invitation to Faith

16.1   GREETING
From Titus 1†

Grace and peace from God our Father
and Jesus Christ our Saviour. **Amen**

16.13   RESPONSE
From Romans 10†

Faith comes from hearing the message:
**and the message is heard
when Christ is proclaimed.**

16.14   RESPONSE
From Ephesians 2†

By grace you have been saved, through
faith – and this not from yourselves, it is
the gift of God – not by works, so that
no-one can boast:
**we are God's workmanship,
created in Christ Jesus
   to do good works,
which God prepared in advance
   for us to do. Amen.**

16.15   RESPONSE
From 2 Corinthians 5†

Anyone who is in Christ is a new
creation:
**the old has passed away –
see, the new has come!**

16.16   RESPONSE
From Colossians 1†

God has rescued us from the power of
darkness, and brought us safe into the
kingdom of his dear Son:
**in Christ our sins are forgiven,.
we are set free. Amen.**

16.17   RESPONSE
From Psalm 34†

Glorify the Lord with me:
let us praise his name together.

16.19   APPROACH
Editors

Our God, we come to you recognising
that we fail; our human flesh is weak,
our sins are many. But we are assured
that sincere confession is met by your
saving forgiveness:

Through your Son our sins are forgiven.
For your mercies:
our God, we thank you.

Our guilt is dealt with, our burdens are
lifted, our lives begin again. For your
mercies:
our God, we thank you.

Through your Spirit we know your

presence, our loneliness is shared; our blind eyes made to see, our love is rekindled. For your mercies:
our God, we thank you.

You and you alone can heal, restore, forgive. Your compassion and your understanding seep into us, your wisdom enlightens us, new courage grips us, and we find your Spirit at work in us bringing together everything which was fractured by our selfishness and sin.
O Lord our God to you be glory
for ever and ever. Amen.

16.21 PRAISE
From Isaiah 12†

The Lord is my strength and my song:
he has become my salvation.

Sing to the Lord, for he has done glorious things:
let it be known through all the world.
Amen.

16.22 PRAISE
Editors

Praise be to God for his promise of pardon:
thanks be to him for his gift of new life!

O Lord release our hearts and minds:
our mouths
will freely praise your name. Amen.

16.23 CONFESSION
Editors

Let us confess our sins to God and ask for his forgiveness:

For all the wrong things we have done: in your mercy,
forgive us, O God.

For forgetting what we ought to have remembered, for failing to do as we promised, for turning away when we should have listened, for being careless when we should have been diligent: in your mercy,
forgive us, O God.

For doing things we knew would annoy, for acting in ways we knew would hurt, for behaving in ways we knew would disappoint: in your mercy,
forgive us, O God.

O God, when we look back
we can see how foolish and wrong
we have been.
Forgive us,
and help us
not to do the same things again;
through Jesus Christ our Lord. Amen.

16.24 CONFESSION
From Ezra 9†

O God,
we are too ashamed and disgraced
to lift up our faces to you,
because our sins
are higher than our heads,
and our guilt has reached
to the heavens.
O Lord you are righteous;
we are before you in our guilt,
not one of us can stand
in your presence.
Forgive us; in Jesus' name. Amen.

16.25 CONFESSION
From Psalm 142†

Lord, we have sinned:
we lift up our voice to you
and cry for your mercy.
There is no-one else to whom we can go:
save us from our sins
and from temptations
that are too strong for us.
Set us free,
that we may praise your name;
through Jesus Christ our Lord. Amen.

16.29 COLLECT
Pentecost 6, ASB 1980

Almighty God,
without you
we are not able to please you.
Mercifully grant that your Holy Spirit
may in all things

→

direct and rule our hearts;
through Jesus Christ our Lord. **Amen.**

16.30 PSALM
Psalm 40.1–3†

I waited patiently for the Lord:
he turned and heard my cry.

He pulled me out of the slimy pit:
out of the mud and mire.

He set my feet upon a rock:
and made my step secure.

He put a new song in my mouth:
a hymn of praise to God.

Many will see it and fear;
and put their trust in the Lord. Amen.

16.32 CREED
From Galatians 2†

**We have been crucified with Christ
and we no longer live,
but Christ lives in us.
The life we live in the body
we live by faith in the Son of God,
who loved us and gave himself for us.
Amen.**

16.33 CREED
From Titus 3†

Let us declare our faith in God's
salvation:

**God our Saviour saved us
not because of righteous things
  we had done,
but because of his mercy.
He saved us
through the washing of rebirth
and renewal by the Holy Spirit,
whom he poured out on us generously
through Jesus Christ our Saviour
so that,
having been justified by his grace,
we might become heirs
having the hope of eternal life.**

This is a trustworthy saying. **Amen.**

16.34 CREED
From 1 Timothy 3†

Beyond all question the mystery of
godliness is great:

**The Son of God appeared in a body,
he was vindicated by the Spirit,
he was seen by apostles,
he was preached among the nations,
he was believed on in the world,
he was taken up to glory. Amen.**

16.38 WE ASK FOR GOD'S
FORGIVENESS
*From 'Contemporary Parish Prayers',
adapted*

Most merciful God and Father,
give us true repentance for our sins.
Open our eyes
to recognise the truth
  about ourselves;
so that acknowledging our faults,
our weaknesses, and our failures,
we may receive your forgiveness,
and find in your love
the encouragement
  to make a new beginning;
for the sake of Jesus Christ our Lord.
Amen.

16.39 THAT WE MAY WALK IN
GOD'S LIGHT
From 1 John 1†

O God, you are light,
and in you there is no darkness at all:
give us grace
no longer to walk in darkness,
but to walk in the light;
to live by the truth,
to have fellowship with you
and with one another,
purified from all sin
by the blood of your Son,
Jesus Christ our Lord. **Amen.**

16.41　FOR SAVING FAITH
From John 3†

Holy Spirit of God,
invisible like the wind,
we do not see you moving among us,
but your effect we see:
come to our hearts
that we may be renewed and reborn.

Open our minds that we may
see your kingdom;
lift up our eyes
to where the cross of Christ stands
for our healing –
that we might believe,
and in believing not die
but have eternal life;
through your Son
who in your love for us
you sent into the world,
Jesus Christ our Lord. **Amen.**

16.42　FOR TRUST IN GOD
Søren Kierkegaard

Teach us, O God
not to torture ourselves,
not to make martyrs of ourselves
　through stifling reflection;
but rather teach us
to breathe deeply in faith,
through Jesus, our Lord. **Amen.**

16.43　FOR ASSURANCE
From Hebrews 11†

Living God,
give us faith
to be sure of what we hope for,
and certain of what we do not see;
to believe that you are,
and that you reward those
　who truly seek you:
so may we please you,
and receive what you have promised;
in Jesus Christ our Lord. **Amen.**

16.45　A PRAYER
　　　　OF INDIVIDUAL FAITH
Maurice Wood

Lord Jesus, my saviour,
my heart is cold,
　warm it by your selfless love,
my heart is sinful,
　cleanse it by your precious blood,
my heart is weak,
　strengthen it by your joyful Spirit,
my heart is empty,
　fill it with your divine presence;
Lord Jesus,
my heart is yours,
possess it always and only for yourself.
Amen.

16.46　COMMITMENT:
　　　　A PERSONAL PRAYER
Editors

Lord Jesus Christ,
I am healed through the prayer of faith,
accepted by you
and drawn to your open arms,
and so I come to you now
　in deep thankfulness.
I receive your gift of salvation
and new life,
and I resolve to live for you
in the power of your Spirit.
Thank you for the new peace in my heart
and for the joy of knowing
that one day I shall see you
in all your heavenly splendour. **Amen.**

16.49　THANKSGIVING
Emmanuel Church, Northwood

Heavenly Father, we come before you
with thanksgiving for all your mercy and
your grace:

For the beauty of the world around us,
we bring you our love,
and give you our thanks and praise.

For our parents and our families, we
bring you our love,
and give you our thanks and praise.

→

For work and play, for food and clothes,
we bring you our love,
and give you our thanks and praise.

For the joy of friends, and for the
happiness we share, we bring you our
love,
and give you our thanks and praise.

But most of all, for your Son Jesus Christ,
for his wonderful birth, for the example
of his life, for his death on the cross to
save us, for raising him from the dead to
be our living Lord, and for sending upon
us your Holy Spirit, we bring you our
love,
and give you our thanks and praise.

**Help us to serve you
gladly and faithfully all our days,
until you call us
to worship you in heaven. Amen.**

16.51 PRAYER OF FAITH
Editors

Our Father in heaven,
we rejoice in the precious name
  of your Son,
the Lord Jesus Christ,
for we have heard
the message of salvation
and we have understood it.
Now we receive Christ into our hearts
  by faith

with joy and thanksgiving.
Jesus, thank you for being our Saviour,
thank you for being our friend:
through your Holy Spirit
we will live for you
and serve you gladly
now and all our days. **Amen.**

16.52 DEDICATION
Editors

Lord Jesus Christ,
we give ourselves into your hands.
Grant us grace to see you,
to know your way,
to feel you near.
Find us now in the quiet,
and hold us fast in the haste of the day;
for your glory's sake. **Amen.**

16.53 DOXOLOGY
From Romans 11†

Oh, the depth of the riches of the wisdom
and knowledge of God!
**How unsearchable his judgements,
and his paths beyond tracing out!**

Who has known the mind of the Lord?
Or who has been his counsellor?
**Who has ever given to God,
that God should repay?**

For from him and through him and to
him are all things.
To God be the glory for ever! Amen.

The Witnessing Church, The Worldwide Church

17.1 GREETING
From Ephesians 6†

Peace to our brothers and sisters, and
love with faith from God the Father and
the Lord Jesus Christ. **Amen.**

17.2 GREETING
From Ephesians 2†

Peace to those who are near, and peace to
those who are far away:
**through Christ
we all can approach the Father
by the one Holy Spirit. Amen.**

17.14 RESPONSE
From John 20†

Jesus said, 'As the Father has sent me I am sending you – receive the Holy Spirit'. **Amen.**

17.15 RESPONSE
From Revelation 11†

The kingdom of the world has become the kingdom of our Lord and of his Christ:
and he will reign for ever and ever. Amen.

17.16 RESPONSE
From Revelation 1†

Jesus Christ has made us to be a kingdom and priests to serve his God and Father:
to him be glory and power for ever and ever. Amen.

17.17 RESPONSE
From Isaiah 48†

With songs of joy proclaim it; tell it to the ends of the earth:
the Lord has set his people free!

17.18 RESPONSE
From 1 Chronicles 16†

Let the heavens rejoice:
let the earth be glad.

Let them say among the people:
the Lord reigns! Amen.

17.20 PRAISE
From Psalm 98†

Sing to the Lord, all the world,
for the Lord is a mighty God.

Sing a new song to the Lord,
for he has done marvellous things.

Proclaim his glory among the nations,
and shout for joy to the Lord our king!

17.21 PRAISE
From Deuteronomy 32†

We will proclaim the name of the Lord:
Oh praise the greatness of our God!

God is the Rock:
**his works are perfect,
and all his ways are just.**

17.22 CONFESSION
Editors

Lord God, our maker and redeemer, this is your world and we are your people: come among us and save us.

Where we have heard for ourselves the good news of Christ, but have not shared it with our generation nor taught it to our children, be merciful:
Lord, forgive us and help us.

Where we have failed to bring the love of Christ to the needy in our society, be merciful:
Lord, forgive us and help us.

Where we have not loved you with all our heart, nor our neighbours as ourselves, be merciful:
Lord, forgive us and help us.

**O God,
forgive us for our lack of love,
and in your mercy make us
what you would have us be,
through Jesus Christ our Lord. Amen.**

17.23 CONFESSION
Alternative Confession, ASB 1980

**Father eternal,
giver of light and grace,
we have sinned against you
in what we have thought,
in what we have said and done,
through ignorance, through weakness,
through our own deliberate fault.
We have wounded your love,
and marred your image in us.**

**We are sorry and ashamed,
and repent of all our sins.**

→

For the sake of your Son Jesus Christ,
  who died for us,
forgive us all that is past;
and lead us out from darkness
to walk as children of light. Amen.

17.25 COLLECT
Pentecost, ASB 1980

Almighty God,
who on the day of Pentecost
sent your Holy Spirit to the disciples
with the wind from heaven
and in tongues of flame,
filling them with joy and boldness
to preach the gospel:
send us out
in the power of the same Spirit
to witness to your truth
and to draw all people
to the fire of your love;
through Jesus Christ our Lord. **Amen.**

17.26 COLLECT
Frank Colquhoun

Heavenly Father,
we thank you
for making us in our baptism
members of your worldwide family
  the Church,
and for our brothers and sisters
in every land
who love the Lord Jesus:
keep us loyal to one another,
faithful to our promises,
and active in your service,
for Jesus Christ's sake. **Amen.**

17.27 PSALM
Psalm 96. 1–13†

The congregation may divide at A and B

  Sing to the Lord a new song:
a **sing to the Lord, all the earth.**

  Sing to the Lord, praise his name:
b **proclaim his salvation each day.**

Declare his glory among the nations:
a **his marvellous deeds among the
  peoples.**

Great is the Lord, and worthy of
  praise:
b **honour him above all gods.**

Splendour and majesty surround
  him:
a **power and beauty fill his temple.**

Praise the Lord all people on earth:
b **praise his glory and might.**

Give him the glory due to his name:
a **bring an offering into his temple.**

Worship the Lord in his beauty and
  holiness:
b **tremble before him all the earth.**

Say to the nations:
ALL **The Lord is king!**

Let the heavens rejoice and the earth
  be glad:
a **let all creation sing for joy.**

For God shall come to judge the
  world:
b **and rule the people with his truth.
  Amen.**

17.29 CREED
From Isaiah 43†

**We believe in the Lord God,
the Holy One,
Father, Son and Holy Spirit;
we are his witnesses and his servants.**

**He alone is the Lord,
apart from him there is no saviour;
he has revealed and saved
and proclaimed;
he is our creator, our redeemer
and our king;
it is he who blots out our transgressions
and remembers our sins no more. Amen.**

17.30 CREED
From 1 Corinthians 8 and 12†

There is one God and Father:
from him all things come.

There is one Lord Jesus Christ:
through him we come to God.

There is one Holy Spirit:
in him we are baptized into one body.

We believe in one God:
Father, Son, and Holy Spirit. Amen.

17.32 FOR HOSTAGES AND
PRISONERS OF CONSCIENCE
Michael Walker, adapted

Lord of all freedom and peace, we pray for the victims of oppressors, for populations who are denied the freedom of political debate and intellectual enquiry, for men, women and children in the prisons and camps of oppressive regimes, and for all hostages.

Those who are in solitary confinement:
merciful Father,
we lift them to you in prayer.

Those who are being tortured:
merciful Father,
we lift them to you in prayer.

Those who have been imprisoned for many years:
merciful Father,
we lift them to you in prayer.

Families who suffer:
merciful Father,
we lift them to you in prayer.

Children of prisoners of conscience:
merciful Father,
we lift them to you in prayer.

Wives and husbands whose years of years of marriage are spent in waiting and praying for the day when prison doors will be opened:
merciful Father,
we lift them to you in prayer.

We pray for all who daily remind us of their plight and whose vigilance knows no rest:
in the name of Christ sustain them.
Amen.

17.33 FOR MISSIONARIES
Michael Botting

Heavenly Father,
we pray for those
who have gone to other countries
with the good news of Jesus:
when their work is difficult and tiring,
make them strong;
when they are lonely and homesick,
remind them that you are with them;
when they are uncertain what to do,
guide them.
Keep them at all times loving you;
for Jesus' sake. **Amen.**

17.36 FOR CHRISTIAN WORKERS
Patricia Mitchell

We thank you Father for your gift of perfect love in Jesus Christ; we offer prayer for all who have accepted that gift and in whom your light shines:

For those who seek to improve the plight of the homeless and badly housed, Father, we thank you:
give them your strength.

For young people sharing their learning and energy freely through voluntary service at home and abroad, Father, we thank you:
give them your strength.

For all organisations helping to relieve suffering and distress in stricken lands, Father, we thank you:
give them your strength.

For missionaries living out your message in the midst of ignorance, fear and disease, Father, we thank you:
give them your strength.

For all those who freely offer time and energy to bring comfort, hope, and help to those in need, Father, we thank you:
give them your strength.

Your light shines on in the darkness,
and the darkness has not overcome it:
for this we thank you, Father,
through Jesus Christ our Lord. Amen.

17.38   FOR TEACHERS
Liturgical Commission

Bless those who teach,
that they may increase
   our understanding,
and be open to your word for them.
Jesus, Lord of your Church:
in your mercy hear us. Amen.

17.40   ABOUT THE GOOD NEWS
From 'A New Zealand Prayer Book'

Everlasting God,
your messengers
have carried the good news of Christ
to the ends of the earth;
grant that
we who commemorate
the builders of your Church
may know the truth of
the gospel in our hearts
and build well on
the foundations they have laid;
through Jesus Christ our Lord. **Amen.**

17.43   FOR CHURCHES AND
            CONGREGATIONS
Unknown, adapted Editors

Lord Jesus, we pray that we may tell and
live your good news wherever people are
found:

That churches in the middle of cities
where people come but do not live,
where commerce and businesses flourish,
may find how they can be effective
centres of witness and worship, Lord,
send your Holy Spirit:
bless your waiting people.

That churches in rural communities'
where all are known to others' may find
true fellowship in their smaller numbers
and, by their lives, be true witnesses to
you, Lord, send your Holy Spirit:
bless your waiting people.

That churches in towns and suburbs,
where houses and work-places mingle,
may provide caring communities for the

lonely and needy to find acceptance,
Lord, send your Holy Spirit:
bless your waiting people.

That all our churches may be centres of
hope and love for those who have lost
their way, or are overburdened with
need, Lord, send your Holy Spirit:
bless your waiting people.

That we all may know his revitalising
power, show holiness of life, and be
ready to share his gifts, Lord, send your
Holy Spirit:
bless your waiting people.

**Hear our prayer which
we offer in the name
   of Jesus Christ our Lord. Amen.**

17.55   FOR US AS GOD'S PEOPLE
Editors

O God, our Father, we ask that you will
give a sense of the important in life:

From the trivial, the self-satisfaction and
smugness with past achievement; from
complacency with our present situation,
Lord, save us:
Lord, in your mercy save us.

From tyranny of non-essentials which
sap our energy, Lord, save us:
Lord, in your mercy save us.

From fear of new methods, especially in
communicating your word, Lord, save
us:
Lord, in your mercy save us.

From lack of imagination in using our
resources with zeal and enthusiasm,
Lord, save us:
Lord, in your mercy save us.

From all distrust of our partners in the
work of your Kingdom, Lord, save us:
Lord, in your mercy save us.

Give us the gifts of patience and courage
in all our living; determination to enjoy
life and wisdom to select those pursuits
which are your will for us. And let your
gifts, so freely given, be used generously
in our varied activities and occupations,

so that others may become aware of your living Spirit and come to share in the life which is abounding and wonderfully fulfilling; even the fellowship of our Saviour, Jesus Christ. **Amen.**

17.56 FOR THE MISSION OF THE CHURCH
From 'A New Zealand Prayer Book'

Draw your Church together, O God;
into one great company of disciples;
together following our Lord Jesus Christ
into every walk of life,
together serving him
in his mission to the world,
and together witnessing to his love
on every continent and island. **Amen.**

17.59 FOR OUR WITNESS TO THE WORLD
Alan Gaunt

Fill us with your love
so that we may gladly
    speak for you,
    work for you,
    and live our whole life for you,
until all the nations of the earth
join with us in endless praise;
through Jesus Christ our Lord. **Amen.**

17.64 ABOUT OUR WITNESS
Michael Botting

O Lord God,
we are all called to be your witnesses:
help us to make Jesus our saviour known
    to others –
through our words and our lives,
through our prayers and our gifts;
for his sake. **Amen.**

17.66 FOR STRENGTH TO WITNESS
From 'A New Zealand Prayer Book'

Almighty Father,
grant that we your children
may never be ashamed
to confess the faith of Christ crucified,
but continue his faithful servants
to our lives' end. **Amen.**

17.67 FOR COURAGE
Editor

Our heavenly Father,
your Son left his glory
    for the sorrow of our world:
grant us the strength
to leave behind our comfort and security,
to take up the cross of our Saviour
and follow where he leads;
for his name's sake. **Amen.**

17.68 TO BE READY
From 'A New Zealand Prayer Book'

Rouse our spirits, Lord Jesus,
that whenever you come to the door
    and knock
you may find us awake,
ready to admit and serve you. **Amen.**

17.70 THANKSGIVING
Editors

Lord God, we thank you for our heritage of faith:

For the vision of apostles and evangelists who brought it to us, gracious Lord,
we give you thanks and praise.

For the courage of martyrs and teachers who secured it for us, gracious Lord,
we give you thanks and praise.

For the devotion of preachers and pastors who proclaimed it to us, gracious Lord,
we give you thanks and praise.

For the love of families and friends who nourished it within us, gracious Lord,
we give you thanks and praise.

For the freedom to speak of it in the world about us, and to share it with our neighbours, gracious Lord,
we give you thanks and praise.

Lord God,
we thank you for our heritage of faith:
give us the will and the strength
to pass it on to others
for glory of your name;
through Jesus Christ our Lord. Amen.

17.71 DEDICATION
Editors

**God our Father,
we dedicate ourselves
to serve you faithfully
and to follow Christ:
send us out to work and to witness
    freely, gratefully and hopefully,
in the power of the Holy Spirit,
and for the honour and glory
    of your Son,
Jesus Christ our Lord. Amen.**

17.72 ASCRIPTION
From Revelation 4†

You are worthy, O Lord our God:
to receive glory and honour and power.

For you created all things:
**and by your will they existed
and were created.**

You are worthy, O Christ, for you were slain:
**and by your blood
you ransomed us for God.**

From every tribe and tongue and people and nation:
**you made us a kingdom of priests
to serve our God.**

To him who sits upon the throne, and to the Lamb:
**be blessing and honour
and glory and might
for ever and ever. Amen.**

17.73 DEDICATION
Liturgical Commission

Send us to tell the world the good news of your healing love; Father, by your Spirit:
bring in your kingdom. Amen.

The Caring Church, Healing

18.1 GREETING
From 1 Peter 5†

Peace to all of you who are in Christ:
let us greet one another with love.

18.7 RESPONSE
From Amos 5†

Let justice flow like a river:
**and righteousness
like a never-failing stream.**

18.8 RESPONSE
From Matthew 20†

The Son of Man did not come to be served, but to serve:
**and to give his life
as a ransom for many.**

18.9 RESPONSE
From Galations 2†

Help to carry one another's burdens:
and so obey the law of Christ. Amen.

18.10 RESPONSE
From 1 John 4

Love one another,
for love is of God,
and whoever loves is born of God
    and knows God:
Spirit of God, search our hearts. Amen.

18.11 FOR HEALING
Editors

O God of peace and Lord of love, help us to be quiet, relaxed and receptive today, accepting the inpouring of yourself, so that in the depths of our nature and being, your healing grace may take from

us any anxious cares, any unworthy thoughts, and all ingratitude:
Forgive us, cleanse us, and renew us, that our hearts may be at rest in you, through Jesus Christ our Saviour. Amen.

18.13 PRAISE
From Psalm 105†

Give thanks to the Lord, call on his name;
**make his deeds known
in the world around.**

Sing to him, sing praise to him;
**tell of the wonderful things
     he has done.**

Glory in his holy name;
**let those who seek the Lord rejoice!
Amen.**

18.14 CONFESSION
Editors

Father, the constancy of your caring love never ceases to amaze us. We confess that our lives are often careless and sometimes loveless.

When our love for you is weak, forgive us:
O God, have mercy.

When our concern for those in need is inadequate, forgive us:
O God, have mercy.

When our giving is meagre and thoughtless, forgive us:
O God, have mercy.

We confess we are often self-centered, and sometimes heartless.

When we distrust the generosity of others, or suspect their motives, forgive us:
O God, have mercy.

When we lack the vision and dedication to bring relief and care to the hungry, the homeless, the displaced person or the refugee, forgive us:
O God have mercy.

**Help us, O God,
to shoulder our responsibilities
in the strength
     of our risen saviour and Lord,
and by your grace
to become agents
     of your transforming love,
for the glory of your name. Amen.**

18.15 CONFESSION
Diocese of Sheffield, adapted

O God our Father, we ask your forgiveness, for we have failed you:

We have not cared enough for your world: in your great mercy:
forgive us, O God.

We have not cared enough for you: in your great mercy,
forgive us, O God.

We have been content with ourselves as we are: in your great mercy,
forgive us, O God.

**Give us the will and the power
to live in the spirit of Jesus,
now and always. Amen.**

18.16 CONFESSION
From 'A New Zealand Prayer Book'

In God there is forgiveness:

**Loving and all-seeing God,
forgive us where we have failed
     to support one another
and to be what we claim to be.
Forgive us where we have failed
     to serve you;
and where our thoughts and actions
have been contrary to your word
we ask your pardon. Amen.**

18.17 CONFESSION
Editor

We confess to you, our heavenly and holy Father, our faltering faith, our foolishness in not following our Lord Jesus Christ more closely, and our failure in Christian living. We have lost opportunities to help and to heal, to comfort and sustain. Give us your strength and pardon our continual mistakes:

**Lord, have mercy on us:
forgive our sins,
and restore us in love
to the service of Jesus Christ our Lord.
Amen.**

18.21 COLLECT
From 'The Gelasian Sacramentary'

O God,
you are the light of the minds
   that know you.
the life of the souls that love you,
and the strength of the wills
   that serve you:
help us so to know you
that we may truly love you,
and so to love you that
we may truly serve you;
whom to serve is perfect freedom;
through Jesus Christ our Lord. **Amen.**

18.22 COLLECT
For the Sick, ASB 1980

Creator and Father of all,
we pray for those who are ill.
Bless them,
and those who serve their needs,
that they may put their whole trust
   in you
and be filled with your peace;
through Jesus Christ our Lord. **Amen.**

18.23 COLLECT
Maundy Thursday 2, ASB 1980

Almighty Father,
whose Son Jesus Christ has taught us
that what we do for the least
   of our brothers and sisters
we do also for him;
give us the will
to be the servant of others
as he was the servant of all,
who gave up his life and died for us,
but is alive and reigns

with you and the Holy Spirit,
one God, now and for ever. **Amen.**

18.24 PSALM
Psalm 103.1–22†

The congregation may divide at A and B

Praise the Lord, my soul:
A **all my being, praise his holy name!**

Praise the Lord, my soul:
B **and do not forget
how generous he is.**

A **He forgives all my sins:**
B **and heals all my diseases.**
A **He keeps me from the grave:**
B **and blesses me
with love and mercy.**

The Lord is gracious and
compassionate:
A **slow to become angry,**
B **and full of constant love.**

He does not keep on rebuking:
A **he is not angry for ever.**

He does not punish us as we
deserve:
B **or repay us for our wrongs.**

As far as the east is from the west:
A **so far does he remove our sins
from us.**

As kind as a Father to his children:
B **so kind is the Lord
to those who honour him.**

Praise the Lord, all his creation:
ALL **praise the Lord, my soul! Amen.**

18.25 PSALM
Psalm 117.1–2†

The congregation may divide at A and B

Praise the Lord, all you nations:
A **praise him, all you people!**

Great is his love towards us:
B **his faithfulness shall last for ever.**

Praise the Lord:
Amen.

18.27 CREED
Diocese of London

Let us declare our faith and trust in God:

Do you believe and trust in God the Father, who made the world and loves it and sustains it?
We believe and trust in him.

Do you believe and trust in God the Son, who came into the world not to be served but to serve, and to give his life as a ransom for many?
We believe and trust in him.

Do you believe and trust in God the Holy Spirit, who fills all creation and who pours out his love in the hearts of those who seek him?
We believe and trust in him.

Will you then constantly ask for the grace of the Holy Spirit, that you may love and serve God, your neighbours and each other, after the example of Christ and in accordance with the Father's will?
By God's help we will. Amen.

18.28 FOR OUR NEIGHBOURS
From 'A New Zealand Prayer Book'

Jesus Christ, you have taught us
that what we do to each other,
we do to you;
make us quick to help and slow to hurt,
knowing that in our neighbour
it is you who receive our love
or our neglect. **Amen.**

18.40 AT A SERVICE OF PRAYER
FOR HEALING
Editors

Lord, hear us as we pray for N. We pray for his healing. May he trust in you and grow in strength and faith:
Jesus, in your mercy, come to heal us;
Jesus, in your mercy, take our pain;
Jesus, special friend of all who suffer,
bless us now, and make us whole again.
Amen.

18.42 FOR THOSE IN NEED
Christopher Idle

Remember, O merciful God,
all those in need;
people with no good food
    or proper clothes,
no home of their own or no work to do,
no family or friends,
no knowledge of your love.
Move us to respond to their plight
and strengthen us to help them;
through Jesus Christ, our Lord. **Amen.**

18.47 FOR OFFENDERS
From 'New Every Morning', adapted

Christ our Lord,
friend of outcasts and sinners:
grant your gift of repentance
to all offenders against the law;
and the knowledge of your forgiveness
to the penitent;
so renew a right spirit within them
that they may find true joy and freedom
in your service. **Amen.**

18.51 HEALING
Editors

Lord, we bring to you . . . :
surround *him* with your love. Amen.

18.52 FOR THOSE WHO HURT
AND THOSE WHO HEAL
Editors

Lord Jesus, we remember those who suffer pain: some physically ill and weary, some nervous, tense and distressed, some with burdens they cannot share with others. All have need of you; we bring their needs before you:
Lord, in your love and mercy,
heal and comfort them.

Lord Jesus, we remember before you those who are disappointed in life: some feeling that life has passed them by, some unwanted and unloved, some unemployed and frustrated, some never having realised their potential. All have

need of you; we bring their needs before you:
**Lord, in your love and mercy,
restore and encourage them.**

Lord Jesus, we pray for those who seek to relieve pain and disappointment: doctors, nurses, and hospice staff; research workers, counsellors, and all who minister to us when we are in need:
**grant them wisdom, strength,
and good success;
so bless your people
to the glory of God the Father. Amen.**

18.54   FOR HEALING
From Jeremiah 17†

O Lord, heal us,
and we shall be healed,
save us,
and we shall be saved:
and the praise shall be yours alone.
Amen.

18.55   FOR HEALING
St Michael-le-Belfrey, York

Merciful Father,
help all who suffer pain of body
or grief of heart,
to find in you their help;
and, as Jesus suffered pain in his body
and healed it in others,
help them to find their peace and healing
    in him;
for his sake. **Amen.**

18.59   FOR THOSE WHO BRING
HEALTH
Editors

We are so grateful, our God, that you have placed us together in life to serve and help one another. We give thanks to you and pray for all who care for the health of our people.

For doctors and surgeons, nurses, technicians and all who combine their skills to help us when we are unwell, Lord, we ask your help:
strengthen and encourage them.

For scientists and researchers who seek new ways and means of combating disease, Lord, we ask your help:
strengthen and encourage them.

For all who play a supportive role in our health services – ambulance crews, administrators, chaplains, catering staff, and all voluntary workers – for these, Lord, we ask your help:
strengthen and encourage them.

For all who bear witness to you as the ultimate healer – for prophets, pastors and preachers, and for individual believers filled with the Father's love, the Saviour's compassion and the Spirit's energy.
**through us, Lord,
work out your great redemption
for the glory of your name. Amen.**

18.61   FOR VISION AND STRENGTH
Editors

O God our Father, who in Jesus came to bring good news to the poor, sight to the blind, freedom to the oppressed, and salvation to your people:

Inspire us to care for each other like brothers and like sisters: Father, by your grace,
help us to love one another.

Send us out to relieve the poor and rescue the oppressed: Father, by your grace.
help us to love one another.

Prepare us to tell the world the good news of your saving love: Father, by your grace,
help us to love one another.

**O God,
make us one in heart and mind,
in the spirit of service,
and in the faith of Jesus Christ our Lord.
Amen.**

18.62 FOR GRACE
Franciscan prayer

Lord, make us instruments of your peace:

Where there is hatred,
let us bring love.

Where there is injury,
let us bring pardon.

Where there is doubt,
let us bring faith.

Where there is despair,
let us bring hope.

Where there is sadness,
let us bring joy.

Where there is darkness,
let us bring light.

O Divine Master, let us seek not so much to be comforted as to comfort, to be understood as to understand, to be loved as to love:
for it is only in giving that we receive, in forgetting ourselves that we find, in pardoning that we are pardoned, in dying that we rise to eternal life; through Jesus Christ our Lord. Amen.

18.63 FOR A SPIRIT OF CARING
St Michael-le-Belfrey, York

O God our Father,
we praise you
that through Jesus Christ your only Son,
you have adopted us
into your family the Church
and made us your children:
help us
to show our love and thanks to you
by care and concern for one another;
use us
to spread your love in all the world
by the power of your Holy Spirit,
and to the honour of your name. **Amen.**

18.67 FOR INSPIRATION TO CARE
From 'A New Zealand Prayer Book'

Save us, Lord, from hurrying away,
because we do not wish to help,
because we know not how to help,
because we dare not.
Inspire us to use our lives
serving others;
through Jesus Christ our Lord. **Amen.**

18.68 FOR HEALING AND LIBERTY
From 'A New Zealand Prayer Book'

We need your healing, merciful God:
give us true repentance.
Some sins are plain to us;
some escape us,
some we cannot face.
Forgive us;
set us free to hear your word to us;
set us free to serve you. **Amen.**

18.70 FOR GOD'S HELP (MORNING)
From 'A New Zealand Prayer Book'

Loving God, thank you for this new day:
thank you for your love and care for us,
thank you for making each of us special;
help us today to be kind to each other.
Amen.

18.71 THANKSGIVING
From 'More Prayers for Today's Church'

We thank you, Father, for your gift of perfect love – for our Saviour Jesus Christ. We thank you for all who loyally serve him, through whom your light shines on your world:

For those who in the name of Christ seek to improve the plight of the homeless and the badly housed:
Father, we thank you.

For young people who share their learning and energy freely through voluntary service at home and abroad:
Father, we thank you.

For all organisations which help to relieve suffering and distress in stricken lands:
Father, we thank you.

For missionaries living out your message in the midst of ignorance, fear and disease:
Father, we thank you. →

For all those who freely give time and energy and money to bring comfort, hope and help to those with needs:
Father, we thank you.

Your light shines in the darkness, and the darkness has not overcome it: thank you, Father, for your light in Jesus Christ our Lord. Amen.

18.72   THANKSGIVING AND
DEDICATION
Editors

Almighty God,
we thank you for your mercy
   and your grace:
you are our light in darkness,
our strength in weakness,
and our comfort in sorrow.
You heal our bodies and our minds;
you ease our pain,
you lift our anxieties
and give us hope.
So fill us with your Spirit's power
that we may take your healing love
to a world in need,
and bring glory to your name:
through Jesus Christ our Lord. **Amen.**

18.73   THANKSGIVING AND
DEDICATION
Editors

We thank God for our mission in Christ, and pledge the service of our lives:

For the vision, courage and enterprise of

your servants in past days and for their acts of kindness and compassion:
thank you, O God.

For what is being achieved through the churches in our day, to the relief of suffering and the betterment of human life:
thank you, O God.

To support the oppressed:
we dedicate ourselves.

To work for justice:
we dedicate ourselves.

To share in Christ's mission and make him known as the Way, the Truth, and the Life:
we dedicate ourselves.

**O God of mercy,
let your kingdom come today. Amen.**

18.75   DEDICATION TO MISSION
Liturgical Commission

Send us to tell the world the good news of your healing love:
**Father, by your Spirit
bring in your kingdom. Amen.**

18.77   ASCRIPTION
From 1 Timothy 1†

Now to the king eternal,
   immortal, invisible,
the only God,
be honour and glory for ever and ever.
Amen.

God's Gifts to the Church, Renewal

19.1   GREETING
From Philippians 4 and Philemon†

The grace of the Lord Jesus Christ be with your spirit. **Amen.**

19.13   RESPONSE
From Romans 12†

In Christ we who are many form one body and each member belongs to all the others:
**we have different gifts,
according to the grace given us.**

19.14 RESPONSE
From 1 Corinthians 12†

There are differing kinds of gifts:
but the same Spirit.

There are differing kinds of service:
but the same Lord.

There are differing ways of working:
but it is God who works in all.

19.15 RESPONSE
From 2 Corinthians 1†

All God's promises are 'Yes!' in Christ,
and through him we reply 'Amen', to the
glory of God:
Amen.

19.16 RESPONSE
From 2 Corinthians 5†

In Christ you are a new creation:
the old has gone,
the new has come. Amen.

19.17 RESPONSE
From 1 Corinthians 6†

Now you are washed, you are sanctified,
you are justified:
in the name of the Lord Jesus Christ
and by the Spirit of our God. Amen.

19.18 RESPONSE
From Ezekiel 47†

I saw water flowing from the temple . . .
it brought God's life and his salvation.
The people sang in joyful praise:
Alleluia, alleluia! Amen.

19.19 RESPONSE FOR
    CHOIR/MINISTERS
From Psalm 135†

Praise the Lord:
praise the name of the Lord.

Praise him, you servants of the Lord who
lead the worship of his house. Here in the
house of our God, praise the Lord:
praise the Lord, for the Lord is good.

Sing praises to his name, for he loves to
hear them:
praise the Lord. Amen.

19.25 APPROACH
Alan Gaunt, adapted

This is the place and this the time; here
and now God waits to break into our
experience: here and now,
let us praise him!

God waits to change our minds, to
change our lives, to change our ways:
here and now,
let us praise him!

God waits to make us see the world and
the whole of life in a new light: here and
now,
let us praise him!

God waits to fill us with hope, joy and
certainty for the future: here and now,
let us praise him!

This is the place as are all places;
this is the time as are all times:
here and now,
let us praise him! Amen.

19.26 PRAISE
From Psalm 66†

Shout with joy to God, all the earth;
sing to the glory of his name!

Come and see what God has done:
how awesome are his works!

Praise our God, all you people;
sound aloud his praise: Amen.

19.27 CONFESSION
Unknown

O God, we come to you in repentance,
conscious of our sins:

When we are self-satisfied, you expose
our failure. Lord, forgive us:
save us and help us.

→

When we are self-assertive you challenge
our pride. Lord, forgive us:
save us and help us.

When we are self-opinionated, you show
us we do not know everything. Lord,
forgive us:
save us and help us.

When we are self-indulgent, you
condemn our greed. Lord, forgive us:
save us and help us.

When we are self-centred, you take our
peace away. Lord, forgive us:
save us and help us.

Give us a new vision of your holiness,
make us worthy to be your people,
and help us to live up to our calling
in Jesus Christ our Lord. Amen.

19.28 CONFESSION
From Psalm 143†

O Lord,
hear our prayer
as we cry for your mercy;
come to help us
in your faithfulness and righteousness.
Do not bring us to judgement,
for no-one is innocent before you.
Answer us now, Lord;
do not hide yourself from us,
show us the way we should go,
rescue us from the enemy.
Teach us to do your will,
and by your good Spirit
lead us in a safe path,
for your name's sake. Amen.

19.29 CONFESSION
Editors

Most loving saviour, Jesus,
have mercy on us, for we have sinned
and this has caused you grief.
We confess to you now,
not because you do not already
know all about us,
but because we are deeply ashamed
and need to admit our wrong-doing
to you.
Have pity and forgive us, dear saviour,

cleanse and refresh us
with your living water;
for our true desire
is to be clean and whole,
walking in your paths of righteousness
always,
for your name's sake. Amen.

19.30 A PERSONAL PRAYER
OF CONFESSION
Editors

Holy Spirit, help me to take an honest
look at myself and ask myself some
questions: do I love God with all my
heart and soul and strength? Do I reflect
the love of Christ in my daily living? Do I
gladly give myself to the service of
others? Is my main desire to abide
always in the love of God?

Holy Spirit,
I admit that I have not always
obeyed your voice:
please forgive me,
and lift me into your light
where I may yield your fruit –
to the glory of God's Kingdom;
through Jesus my Saviour. Amen.

19.31 CONFESSION
Alan Gaunt

For all our confessions of faith which
have led to nothing, Lord, forgive us:
forgive us and help us.

For all our protestations of love to each
other and to you which have come to
nothing, Lord, forgive us:
forgive us and help us.

For all our chasing after dreams and
striving after schemes which have
achieved nothing, Lord, forgive us:
forgive us and help us.

Teach us to put our faith in you
rather than in ourselves;
so that loving you
we may love each other
with transforming, creative love
like that of Jesus Christ our Lord.
Amen.

19.32 CONFESSION
From Jonah 2†

O Lord our God,
in distress we call to you;
from the depths we cry for help –
the storm swirls around us,
our troubles threaten to engulf us.
We feel we have been banished
 from your sight,
but we look again
towards your loving peace.
We have clung to worthless things
and forfeited the grace
 that could have been ours:
We are trapped under a weight of sin,
and our life in you is ebbing away.
O Lord, we call to you:
forgive us and restore us,
through Jesus our redeemer. Amen.

19.36 COLLECT
Pentecost 6, ASB 1980

Almighty God,
without you
we are not able to please you.
Mercifully grant that your Holy Spirit
may in all things
direct and rule our hearts;
through Jesus Christ our Lord. **Amen.**

19.37 PSALM
Psalm 143.6–10, and Psalm 51.6–12†

*Psalms 143 and 51 have been grouped
together to provide for an occasion when the
person and work of the Holy Spirit is being
considered.*

O Lord, I spread my hands out to you:
I thirst for you like dry ground.

Teach me to do your will, for you are my
God:
let your good Spirit lead me in safety.

You require sincerity and truth in me:
fill my mind with your wisdom.

Create in me a pure heart, O God:
and renew a faithful spirit in me.

Do not cast me from your presence:
or take your Holy Spirit from me.

Give me again the joy of your salvation:
and make me willing to obey. Amen.

19.38 PSALM
Psalm 150. 1–6†

The congregation may divide at A and B

 Praise the Lord!

 Praise God in his sanctuary:
 **praise his strength
  beyond the skies!**

 Praise him for his acts of power:
 A **praise him
  for his surpassing greatness.**

 Praise him with the sounding of the
 trumpet:
 B **praise him with the harp and lyre.**

 Praise him with tambourine and
 dancing:
 A **praise him
  with the strings and flute.**

 Praise him with the clash of cymbals:
 B **praise him with
  resounding cymbals.**

 Let everything that has breath praise
 the Lord:
 ALL **Praise the Lord! Amen.**

19.40 RESPONSE
 (AFTER A READING)
From Revelation 2 and 3†

Hear what the Spirit is saying to the
Church.
Thanks be to God. Amen.

19.41 CREED
From 1 Corinthians 12†

Let us affirm our faith in the unity and
the diversity of God:

**We believe in the one Holy Spirit
giver of gifts of various kinds.**

**We believe in one Jesus Christ
Lord of various kinds of service.**

→

We believe in one almighty Father
working in various ways.

We believe in one God
Father, Son and Holy Spirit. Amen.

19.43   PRAISING THE LORD
Editors

Lord God, our loving heavenly Father,
we speak your praise, for you are ever
faithful. Your mercy is from eternity to
eternity.

For your love, which never wearies or
grows old or becomes indifferent, but is
fresh with each new day, we praise you:
Alleluia! Amen.

You have made all things by your power,
you rule all things in your wisdom. For
the richness of creation and for the mercy
and   grace   which   sustains   and
strengthens us, we thank you:
Alleluia! Amen.

You are always bringing order and
beauty out of chaos and confusion. For
taking the broken fragments of our lives
and knitting them together into renewed
wholeness, we praise you:
Alleluia! Amen.

For your continuing grace of forgiveness,
and for the constant enrichment of your
Holy Spirit, we thank you:
Alleluia! Amen.

We can never restrict your gifts of music,
beauty, art or love, or imprison your
enriching spiritual gifts – to limit them is
to lose your power, to use them selfishly
brings spiritual impoverishment. For all
these your gifts we praise you:
Alleluia! Amen.

We come to you today full of expectation
of your continuing mercy, love and
provision:
**For yours is the kingdom,
the power and the glory for ever.**

Receive our praises,

hear our prayers,
be present through your Spirit
in the name of Jesus Christ our Lord.
Amen.

19.44   FOR MERCY
From Psalm 143†

O Lord,
hear our prayer as we cry for your mercy;
in your faithfulness and righteousness
come to help us.
Do not bring us to judgement,
for no-one is innocent before you.

We remember days gone by,
and think about all you have done for us;
we lift our hands to you in prayer
and our souls thirst for you.
Answer us now, Lord,
don't hide yourself from us;
remind us each morning
    of your constant love,
for we put our trust in you.

We pray to you:
show us the way we should go;
rescue us from the enemy,
teach us to do your will,
by your good spirit
lead us in the right path,
for your name's sake. **Amen.**

19.45   THANKSGIVING
        (MUSICAL SERVICE)
From Psalm 150†

**Here the instruments being used in the
service may be named*

O God, we praise you:

We praise you in your sanctuary:
we praise you in your mighty heaven.

We praise you for your acts of power:
**we praise you
for your surpassing greatness.**

With . . . *, we praise you:
**with every breath
your people praise you.**

We praise you, O God:
Amen. Amen.

19.46 INVOCATION
From 'A New Zealand Prayer Book'

Come, Holy Spirit, with the new fire;
when our prayer seems to fail,
when we hear no voice nor any answer,
rouse us and light our way. **Amen.**

19.53 FOR LIBERTY
IN GOD'S FAMILY
From 'A New Zealand Prayer Book'

Loving God,
in Jesus you gather us into your family;
confidently we call you Father:
may your Spirit bring us to share
the glorious liberty of your children,
now and for ever. **Amen.**

19.55 AT A MUSICAL OCCASION
Editors

God, our creator:
thank you for music and musicians,
thank you for the creation of new songs
   and hymns,
thank you for your Holy Spirit,
who fills our hearts with joy
when we sing melodies of praise to you;
in Jesus' name. **Amen.**

19.57 FOR THE BODY OF CHRIST
Editors

O God our Father, you grant your people
gifts, that we may work together in the
service of your Son:

Bless those who lead, that they may be
strong and true, yet be humble before
you: Lord, through your Spirit,
answer our prayer.

Bless those who teach, that they may
enlighten our understanding, yet be
taught by your wisdom: Lord, through
your Spirit,
answer our prayer.

Bless those who offer healing, that they
may extend your touch of grace, yet
always know your healing presence:
Lord, through your Spirit,
answer our prayer.

Bless those through whom you speak,
that they may proclaim your word in
power, yet have their ears open to your
gentle whisper: Lord, through your
Spirit,
answer our prayer.

Bless those who administer, help, and
organise, that they may be diligent in
their duty, yet seek your kingdom first:
Lord, through your Spirit,
answer our prayer.

Grant that as one Body
we may grow up into him
who is the head of the Church,
even Jesus Christ our Lord. Amen.

19.58 FOR CHURCH FAMILY LIFE
Unknown

Look upon us, O Lord,
and grant us
the grace of your Holy Spirit:
where there is weakness,
give us strength;
where there is disagreement,
give us tolerance;
where there is misunderstanding,
give us patience,
and where there is hurt,
give us the courage to forgive
and the grace to accept forgiveness;
through Jesus Christ our Lord. **Amen.**

19.61 FOR OUR RENEWAL
Epiphany 4, ASB 1980

Almighty God,
in Christ you make all things new:
transform the poverty of our nature
by the riches of your grace;
and in the renewal of our lives
make known your heavenly glory;
through Jesus Christ our Lord. **Amen.**

**19.63   FOR RENEWAL OF HEART
               AND MIND**
From Psalm 51†

Lord, you require in us
sincerity and truth:
fill our minds with your wisdom,
make us happy in your service;
create in us a new heart
and put a loyal spirit in us.
Do not banish us from your presence,
or take your holy spirit from us;
give us the joy
that comes from your salvation,
and make us willing to obey you
through Jesus Christ our Lord. **Amen.**

**19.64   RENEWAL:
               A PERSONAL PRAYER**
Editors

Lord, help me to forget myself,
but never let me forget you;
save me from self-pity,
but give me true compassion for others;
deliver me from self-seeking,
but instil in me the desire to find you;
keep me from being self-willed,
but make me always keen
    to obey your will.
Christ, King of Love, live in me. **Amen.**

19.66   RENEWAL: FOR MISSION
Editors

Lord, call us from the world
to cleanse, teach and equip us.
Then send us back again
to love, serve, and tell the good news
    that you are the Christ,
the sacrificial Lamb of God,
the Resurrection and the Life,
the Holy One, the Almighty,
the Alpha and Omega. **Amen.**

**19.67   FOR A DEEPER LIFE
               IN THE SPIRIT**
Editors

Holy Spirit of God, you are continually
transforming life and always giving us
grace to follow the Lord Jesus Christ.

We pray for the blessing of faith which
expects new truth to break into our
minds:
Lord, give us faith.

We pray for the blessing of strength to
explore the new life which we have
received in Christ Jesus:
Lord, give us strength.

We pray for the blessing of hope, that we
may conquer our doubts and believe in
the power of your good news:
Lord, give us hope.

We pray for the blessing of love that is
patient and kind: break down our self-
seeking and unforgiving spirit. Help us
to delight in the happiness of others and
to rejoice in another's success as much as
in our own:
Lord, give us love.

**O Holy Spirit of God,
deepen our experience
    of your transforming power
through Jesus Christ our Lord. Amen.**

19.68   FOR RENEWAL IN THE SPIRIT
From Ephesians 4 and Colossians 3, Editors

Lord, our God, by the power of your
Holy Spirit cleanse us and strengthen us;
help us to put off the old and put on the
new.

Help us to put off deception and put on
truth,
by the power of your Holy Spirit.

Help us to put off impurity and put on
holiness,
by the power of your Holy Spirit.

Help us to put off malice and put on
forgiveness,
by the power of your Holy Spirit.

Help us to put off anger and put on
peace,
by the power of your Holy Spirit.

Help us to put off coldness and put on
compassion,
by the power of your Holy Spirit.

Help us to put off greed and put on generosity,
by the power of your Holy Spirit.

Help us to put off doubt and put on faith,
by the power of your Holy Spirit.

Help us to put off darkness and put on Light,
by the power of your Holy Spirit.

In the name of Christ who shines upon us.
Amen.

19.73   FOR HEALING AND LIBERTY
From 'A New Zealand Prayer Book'

We need your healing, merciful God:
give us true repentance.
Some sins are plain to us;
some escape us,
some we cannot face.
Forgive us;
set us free to hear your word to us;
set us free to serve you. **Amen.**

19.74   FOR HEALING:
            A PERSONAL PRAYER
Editors

Lord Christ, Son of God:
come to me and cleanse me from my sin;
come to me and heal me
by the power of your Spirit,
come to me and liberate me
    with your love.
So, through your grace
    may I bring comfort
to my sisters and brothers
and lead them into the security
    of your glorious light. **Amen.**

19.76   THANKSGIVING
Emmanuel Church, Northwood

We give thanks to God for all his gifts to us:

For birth and life and strength of body,
for safety and shelter and food: we give you thanks, O God,
and praise your holy name.

For sight and hearing and the beauty of nature, for words and music and the power of thought: we give you thanks, O God,
and praise your holy name.

For work and leisure and the joy of achieving, for conscience and will and depth of feeling: we give you thanks, O God,
and praise your holy name.

For grace and truth in Jesus Christ, for the gifts of the Spirit and the hope of heaven: we give you thanks, O God,
and praise your holy name.

We shall not forget
that you are our God,
and we are your people,
in Jesus Christ our Lord. Amen.

19.77   THANKSGIVING:
            A PERSONAL PRAYER
Editors

Lord Jesus Christ,
you are the Alpha and the Omega,
the bright morning star,
the resurrection and the life,
the Light of the world
and yet you know me.
Thank you, Lord;
thank you for touching my heart
    with your love. **Amen.**

19.79   DEDICATION
Editors

Lord Christ, our Master,
purify us
by the kindling of your Holy Spirit,
and let the unquenchable flame
of your love
burn within us every day,
so that we never forget you. **Amen.**

19.80   DEDICATION: A PERSONAL
          PRAYER
Editors

Lord Jesus Christ, I am healed through
the prayer of faith, accepted by you and
drawn to your open arms, and so I come
to you now in deep thankfulness. I
receive your gift of Salvation and new
life, and I resolve to live for you in the
power of your Spirit. Thank you for the
new peace in my heart and for the joy of
knowing that one day I shall see you in
all your heavenly splendour. **Amen.**

The Local Church: Anniversary, Commitment, Giving

20.1   GREETING
From 1 Corinthians 1†

*Here the local name is supplied.

To the church of God in . . .*, to those
sanctified in Christ Jesus and called to be
holy, to all those everywhere who call on
the name of our Lord Jesus Christ – their
Lord and ours: grace and peace to you
from God our Father and the Lord Jesus
Christ. **Amen.**

20.2   GREETING (EVENING)
From Psalm 134†

All of you who serve the Lord; you who
come in the evening of the day to
worship in his house, you who lift up
your hands in his holy place and praise
the Lord: (may) the Lord, the maker of
heaven and earth, bless you! **Amen.**

20.14   RESPONSE
From Psalm 30†

Sing praise to the Lord, all his faithful
people:
**Remember what the Holy One has done
and give him thanks! Amen.**

20.15   RESPONSE
From Revelation 1†

Jesus has made us a kingdom of priests
to serve his God and Father:
**to him be glory and power
for ever and ever. Amen.**

20.16   RESPONSE
From Ephesians 2†

Jesus Christ is the chief cornerstone:
**in him we are being built together
    into a temple
in which God lives by his Spirit. Amen.**

20.17   RESPONSE
From Hebrews 12†

Let us thank God because we have
received a kingdom which cannot be
shaken:
**let us be grateful
and worship him
in a way that will please him –
with reverence and awe. Amen.**

20.18   RESPONSE
From 2 Corinthians 1†

As surely as God is faithful, no matter
how many promises he has made they
are 'yes' in Christ:
to the glory of God. Amen.

20.19   RESPONSE
From Ezekiel 47†

I saw water flowing from the temple . . .
it brought God's life and his salvation.
The people sang in joyful praise:
Alleluia, alleluia! Amen.

20.20 EVENING
       EXHORTATION/WELCOME
From Psalm 134†

All of you who serve the Lord:
praise the Lord.

You who come in the evening of the day
to worship in his house:
praise the Lord.

Lift up your hands in his holy place:
praise the Lord.

May the Lord, the maker of heaven and
earth, bless you here; through our
Saviour, Jesus Christ. **Amen.**

20.24 PRAISE
From Psalm 150†

Praise God in his sanctuary;
praise him in his mighty heavens.

Praise him for his acts of power;
praise him for his surpassing greatness

Let everything that has breath
   praise the Lord:
praise the Lord! Amen!

20.26 CONFESSION
From 1 Corinthians 13†

Let us confess our lack of love, and our
need of grace:

When we lose patience,
when we are unkind,
when we are envious,
when we are rude or proud,
when we are selfish or irritable,
and when we will not forgive:
have mercy on us, O God.

Help us not to delight in evil,
but to rejoice in the truth;
help us always to protect, to trust,
to hope and to presevere
so that we may see you face to face,
and learn to love as you love us
in Jesus Christ our Lord. Amen.

20.27 CONFESSION
From 'The Promise of His Glory'

Most merciful God,
we confess that we have sinned
   against you
in thought, and word, and deed.
We are truly sorry for our pride,
and for our lack of faith,
of understanding and of love;
We repent of our narrow-mindedness,
of our bitterness and our prejudices.
Pardon and forgive us,
save us and renew us,
that we may delight in your will
and walk in your ways;
through Jesus Christ our Lord. Amen.

20.29 COLLECT
*Dedication/Consecration of a Church, ASB
1980*

Almighty God,
to whose glory we celebrate
the *dedication/consecration*
of this house of prayer:
we praise you for the many blessings
you have given
to those who worship here;
and we pray
that all who seek you in this place
may find you,
and being filled with the Holy Spirit
may become a living temple
acceptable to you;
through Jesus Christ our Lord. **Amen.**

20.30 COLLECT
For a Synod, ASB 1980

Almighty God,
you have given your Holy Spirit
   to the church
that he may lead us into all truth.
Bless with his grace and presence
the leaders of this church;
keep them steadfast in faith
and united in love,
that they may reveal your glory
and prepare the way of your kingdom;
through Jesus Christ our Lord. **Amen.**

20.31 PSALM
Psalm 100.1–5†

The congregation may divide at A and B

Rejoice in the Lord, all the earth:
worship the Lord with gladness.

Remember the Lord is our God:
we are his flock and he made us.

Come to his temple with praise:
enter his gates with thanksgiving.

The love of the Lord will not fail:
God will be faithful for ever. Amen.

20.32 PSALM
Psalm 118.1–29†

M – minister, W – worshipper – from doorway, then moving through congregation, C – choir/chorus, D – director – in matter-of-fact tone.

M Give thanks to the Lord, for he is good:
his love endures for ever.

M All those who fear the Lord shall say:
His love endures for ever.

W Open for me the gates of the Temple; I will go in and give thanks to the Lord.

M This is the gate of the Lord, only the righteous can come in.

W I will give thanks because you heard me; you have become my salvation.

C **The stone
which the builders rejected
    as worthless
turned out to be
    the most important of all:**

   **The Lord has done this – what a
       wonderful sight it is!**

W This is the day of the Lord's victory –
let us be happy, let us celebrate:
**O Lord save us –
O Lord, grant us success.**

M May God bless the one who comes in the name of the Lord:
**The Lord is God –
he has been good to us!**

C From the Temple of the Lord, we bless you.

D With branches in your hands, start the procession and march round the altar:

W You are my God and I will give you thanks:
You are my God, and I will exalt you.

M Give thanks to the Lord, for he is good:
His love endures for ever. Amen.

20.33 PSALM
Psalm 134.1–3†

You servants of the Lord, who stand in his temple at night:
praise the Lord!

Lift your hands in prayer to the Lord:
in his sanctuary, praise the Lord!

May the Lord who made the heaven and earth bless you from Zion:
Amen!

20.37 CREED
From Colossians 1†

Let us confess our faith in the Son of God:

**Christ is the image of the invisible God,
the firstborn over all creation.
By him all things were created:
things in heaven and on earth,
visible and invisible,
thrones, powers, rulers, and authorities;
all things were created by him
    and for him.**

**He is before all things
and in him all things hold together.**

**He is the head of the body, the Church;
he is the beginning
and the firstborn from the dead. Amen.**

20.38   CREED
From Revelation 1†

We believe in God almighty,
the Lord, the first and the last,
who is, who was and who is to come.

We believe in Jesus Christ,
the faithful witness,
the first to be raised from death,
the ruler of the kings of the earth:
he loves us,
and by his sacrificial death
he has freed us from our sins
and made us a kingdom of priests
to serve our God and Father. Amen.

20.39   ACT OF PRAISE
Editors

For your living church, that world-wide
concourse of people who you have
graciously called to be your people; this
day, O God:
we adore you
and praise your holy name.

That you are enthroned in heaven, and
that your rule extends through all
creation; this day, O God:
we adore you
and praise your holy name.

For your consistent goodness and
gentleness and for your constant love and
kindness to us and to everyone; this day,
O God:
we adore you
and praise your holy name.

That in Christ you freely forgive those
who are penitent, and offer your pardon
to sinners; this day, O God:
we adore you
and praise your holy name.

That Jesus lived, died and rose again to
redeem us and make us your own people;
this day, O God:
we adore you
and praise your holy name.

We rejoice this day in your promises
fulfilled in us, and for the hope of life
everlasting.
May your will be done on earth,
as it is in heaven. Amen.

20.40   FOR THE CHURCH OF CHRIST
From BCP Episcopal Church USA

For the holy Church of God, that it may
be filled with truth and love, and be
found without fault at the day of his
coming, let us pray to the Lord:
Lord, have mercy. Amen.

20.44   FOR PATIENCE
Christopher Idle

Grant, our Father,
that in this church
the younger may respect the traditions
   of the older,
and the older may understand
   the impatience of the younger;
so that young and old
may share together in your service,
and gladly recognise
that all are one in Jesus Christ. **Amen.**

20.45   ABOUT OUR STEWARDSHIP
Michael Botting

Lord Jesus Christ,
you have taught us
that we cannot love both God
   and money,
and that all our possessions
are a trust from you:
teach us to be faithful stewards
of our time, our talents, and our money,
that we may help others
   extend your kingdom;
for your name's sake. **Amen.**

20.47 PROMISES/THANKSGIVING
From Revelations 2†

Hear the promises of Jesus, the first and the last, the living one, who was dead but now is alive for ever and ever, who has authority over death and the world of the dead:

Those who win the victory will eat from the tree of life:
thank you, Lord Jesus.

Those who win the victory will not be hurt by the second death:
thank you, Lord Jesus.

Those who win the victory will receive a new name:
thank you, Lord Jesus.

Those who win the victory will receive authority from the Father:
thank you, Lord Jesus.

Those who win the victory will be clothed in white, and their names not removed from the book of the living:
thank you, Lord Jesus. Amen.

20.48 DEDICATION
Liturgical Commission

God and Father,
whose Son our Lord Jesus Christ was rich yet became poor for our sake,
to make us rich out of his poverty;
by your grace let our lives overflow
in a wealth of generous service
to you and to our neighbour;
through the same Jesus Christ our Lord.
Amen.

20.49 AFTER INTERCESSION
From 'A New Zealand Prayer Book'

Those things, good Lord,
that your servants have prayed for,
give us grace to work for;
and in the purpose of your love
answer our prayers and fulfil our hopes
for Jesus' sake. **Amen.**

20.50 THANKSGIVING
        FOR OUR HERITAGE
Editors

We thank God for every gracious influence of godly people:

For parents who were examples of the spiritual truths they believed: with grateful hearts,
our God, we bring you thanks.

For teachers who loved, taught and trained us: with grateful hearts,
our God, we bring you thanks.

For patterns of worship, in music, word and action: with grateful hearts,
our God, we bring you thanks.

For customs of practice and ministry: with grateful hearts.
our God, we bring you thanks.

Help us not to deny our heritage,
remind us that you are the giver
of every good and perfect gift,
and strengthen us
that we may offer ourselves
for your service,
to the glory of your name. Amen.

20.51 THANKSGIVING: CONCLUSION
From Ephesians 5

We give thanks for everything
to God the Father
in the name of our Lord Jesus Christ.
Amen.

20.52 ACT OF DEDICATION
Editors

Lord God, holy Father, since you have called us through Christ to share in a gracious Covenant, we take upon ourselves afresh the yoke of obedience. And, for love of you, we engage ourselves in the task of witness to our neighbours and service to them in your name; each of us saying:

I am no longer my own, but yours –
send me where you will,
rank me with whom you will;

let me be employed for you,
or laid aside for you;
exalted for you,
or brought low for you;
let me be full, let me be empty;
let me have all things,
let me have nothing.

Freely and wholeheartedly
I yield my life and all I possess
to your pleasure and disposal. Amen.

20.53   PRAYER OF DEDICATION
Editors

We offer to God our skills and our
service, our lives and our worship:

O God, you have given us life and health
and strength, and in Jesus Christ you
have given us a saviour and a friend.

For the love that made you enter our
world in Jesus to share our joys and
sorrows and to die for our sin: Father,
receive the gift of our love.

For the forgiveness you promise to all
who confess their sins and trust in his
sacrifice on the cross: Father,
receive the gift of our penitence.

For the hope of eternal life we have in
Christ because you raised him from the
dead: Father,
receive the gift of our lives.

For the blessing of friendship and the
satisfaction of working together, for the
stretching of mind and the exercise of
body: Father,
receive the gift of our service.

Because you are the Lord of all, yet your
ears are open to our cry; and because we
delight to praise you: Father,
receive the gift of our worship.

**Holy, holy, holy Lord,
God of power and might
heaven and earth
are full of your glory.
Hosanna in the highest. Amen.**

20.55   FOR OBEDIENCE
Liturgical Commission

Lord Jesus Christ,
Son of the living God;
teach us to walk in your way
    more trustfully,
to accept your truth more faithfully,
to share your life more lovingly;
so that we may come
by the power of the Holy Spirit
as one family
to the kingdom of the Father
where you live for ever and ever. **Amen.**

20.56   OFFERTORY PRAYER
Stanley Pritchard

Heavenly Father,
let these gifts go where we cannot go,
and help those whom we cannot reach;
through them
let the unlearned be taught,
the hungry fed,
the sick healed,
and the lost found;
for Jesus' sake. **Amen.**

20.57   GOING OUT FROM WORSHIP
Michael Botting, adapted

Be with us, O God,
as we go out in your name:
may the lips that have sung your praises
always speak the truth;
may the ears
    which have heard your word
listen only to what is good;
and may our lives as well as our worship
be always pleasing to you,
for the glory of Jesus Christ our Lord.
Amen.

20.58   DEDICATION
Editors

Father, we dedicate ourselves
to serve you faithfully
and to follow Christ,
to face the future with him,

→

seeking his special purpose
for our lives.
Send us out now to work
and to witness
freely, gratefully and hopefully,
in the power of the Holy Spirit,
and for the honour and glory
of your Son,
Jesus Christ our Lord. **Amen.**

20.59   DEDICATION
Traditional

O God,
strengthen your servants
with your heavenly grace,
that we may continue yours for ever,
and daily increase in your Holy Spirit
more and more,
until we come
to your everlasting kingdom. **Amen.**

20.60   DEDICATION
Sarum Primer, 1527

God be in my head
and in my understanding,

God be in my eyes and in my looking,
God be in my mouth
and in my speaking,
God be in my heart and in my thinking,
God be at my end and at my departing.
Amen.

20.61   ASCRIPTION
From Ephesians 3†

Now to God the Father
who is able to do immeasurably more
than all we ask or think
because the Spirit's power
is at work in us:
to him be glory in the Church
and in Christ Jesus
throughout all generations
for ever and ever! **Amen.**

20.62   BLESSING
From Psalm 128†

The blessing of the Lord be upon *you*:
we bless you in the name of the Lord.
Amen.

Harvest Thanksgiving

21.1   GREETING
From Philemon 1†

Grace to you and peace from God our
Father and the Lord Jesus Christ. **Amen.**

21.8   RESPONSE
From Psalm 67†

The land has yielded its harvest:
God, our God, has blessed us.

God *has* blessed us:
let everyone everywhere honour him!
Amen.

21.9   RESPONSE
From Joel 2†

We have plenty to eat and are satisfied:
Praise the Lord our God
who has done wonderful things. Amen.

21.10   APPROACH
The congregation's responses to the
minister's prayer:

Today, O Lord, we thank you:
and rejoice together in your love.

At the end:
In response to all these,
your many and rich blessings:
today we celebrate your faithfulness
and honour you
with our harvest thanksgiving. Amen.

21.11 PRAISE
From Psalm 103†

Praise the Lord, O my soul
and do not forget his blessings.

He crowns us with his love
and satisfies our need.

21.12 CONFESSION
Editor

O God our Father, we confess that we
have often used your gifts carelessly, and
acted as though we were not grateful.
Hear our prayer, and in your mercy
forgive us and help us:

When we enjoy the fruits of the harvest,
but forget they come from you – then,
Father, in your mercy,
forgive us and help us.

When we are full and satisfied, but
ignore the cry of the hungry and those in
need – then, Father, in your mercy,
forgive us and help us.

When we are thoughtless, and do not
treat with respect or care the wonderful
world you have made – then, Father, in
your mercy,
forgive us and help us.

When we store up goods for ourselves
alone, as if there were no God and no
heaven – then, Father, in your mercy,
forgive us and help us.

Grant us thankful hearts
and a loving concern for all people;
through Jesus Christ our Lord. Amen.

21.13 CONFESSION
Editor

Lord God of plenty, forgive us that
though we live in a rich world we so
often tolerate poverty.

Children die through our indifference:
forgive us, good Lord.

Young people are deprived because of
inherited selfishness:
forgive us, good Lord.

Men and women are embittered by
injustice or poverty:
forgive us, good Lord.

Stir us to consider our priorities,
strengthen our wills to
    examine the way we live,
guide all who make political decisions
    which affect the poor:
in the name of him
who, though he was rich,
yet for our sakes became poor
that we, through his poverty,
might become rich;
Jesus Christ, our Lord. Amen.

21.14 CONFESSION
From Isaiah 43†

O Lord our God,
we confess
    that we have not called upon you,
nor have we tried hard to serve you;
we have not given to you
    from our wealth,
nor have we honoured you
    with the work of our hands;
but we have burdened you
    with our sins,
and wearied you with our wrongdoing:
blot out our transgressions
and remember our sin no more,
for your name's sake. Amen.

21.16 COLLECT
Harvest, ASB 1980

Almighty and everlasting God,
we offer you our hearty thanks
for your fatherly goodness and care
in giving us the fruits of the earth
  in their seasons.
Give us grace to use them rightly,
  to your glory,
    for our own well-being,
    and for the relief of those in need;
through Jesus Christ our Lord. **Amen.**

21.17 COLLECT
Rogation Days, ASB 1980

Almighty God,
you have provided
the resources of the world
to maintain the life of your children,
and have so ordered our life
that we are dependent
   upon each other.
Bless us all in our daily work
and, as you have given us
   the knowledge to produce plenty
so give us the will
to bring it within reach of all;
through Jesus Christ our Lord. **Amen.**

21.18 PSALM
Psalm 65.1–13†

The congregation may divide at A and B.

   O God,
      it is right for us to praise you,
      because you answer our prayers:

   You care for the land and water it:
A **and make it rich and fertile.**

   You fill the running streams with
   water:
B **and irrigate the land.**

   You soften the ground with showers:
A **and make the young crops grow.**

   You crown the year with goodness:
B **and give us a plentiful harvest.**

   The pastures are filled with flocks:
A **the hillsides are clothed with joy.**

   The fields are covered with grain:
ALL **they shout for joy and sing. Amen.**

21.23 CREED
Alternative Service Book 1980, adapted

**We believe and trust in God the Father
who made the world.**

**We believe and trust
   in his Son Jesus Christ,
who redeemed mankind.**

**We believe and trust in his Holy Spirit,
who gives life to the people of God.**

**We believe and trust in one God:
Father, Son, and Holy Spirit. Amen.**

21.24 A HARVEST CREED
From Psalm 65†

We believe in one God who answers our
prayers:

Has he given us victory and done
wonderful things to save us?
He has!

Did he set the mountains in place by his
strength, and calm the roar of the seas?
He did!

Do his deeds bring shouts of joy from
one end of the earth to the other?
They do!

Does he make the land rich and fertile;
does he fill the streams with water, and
provide the earth with crops; does he
send rain on the fields and soften the soil
with showers and make the young plants
grow; does he fill the pastures with
herds; does he cover the hills with sheep,
and the valleys with golden wheat?
He does!

Do his people shout and sing for joy?
We do! Amen.

21.25 OFFERING
        AT LAMMAS/HARVEST
D. L. Couper, adapted

In the name of the farmers and
farmworkers of . . . , we come to offer
our gifts to God in thanksgiving for his
blessing [and to pray for our harvest].

We bring before you, O Lord, this sheaf,
the first-fruits of our harvest, in token of
the gratitude in our hearts.
Blest be God for ever.

We bring before you, O Lord, this loaf,
made from the first ears of the ripe corn,
in humble acknowledgement of our
dependence on all your gifts.
Blest be God for ever.

We bring before you Lord this token of
the wealth that you have given us, and

with it we offer the love of our hearts and the service of our lives.
Yours, Lord, is the greatness, the power, the glory, the splendour, and the majesty; for everything in heaven and on earth is yours. All things come from you, and of your own do we give you. Amen.

21.26   OFFERING AT HARVEST
From Genesis 33†

Spoken by a member of the congregation to the Minister of the church

M , please accept these gifts
   which we have brought:
God has been kind to us
and given us everything we need.
Amen.

21.34   THANKSGIVING
D L Couper

For the rich soil of the countryside, for good seed, and for the green corn springing out of the earth, we thank you O God,
and praise your holy name.

For the warm sweetness of the fertile rain, for the hot days of ripening sun, and for the harvest, we thank you O God,
and praise your holy name.

For the yield of the forests, the earth and the sea, we thank you O God,
and praise your holy name.

For all who work on the land, in the mines, or on the waters, and for their courage in days of difficulty and disappointment, we thank you O God,
and praise your holy name.

For those who work in office, shop, factory or in transport, to meet our needs, we thank you O God,
and praise your holy name.

For these and all your blessings we make

our harvest thanksgiving and give you all the glory:
Glory to the Father, and to the Son, and to the Holy Spirit, as it was in the beginning, is now, and shall be for ever. Amen.

21.35   THANKSGIVING FOR THE HARVEST
Christopher Idle

We thank you, God,
for the harvest of all good things:
for making plants to grow in the earth,
for giving farmers strength to work,
for supplying the food we have each day.
Teach us to use your gifts fairly
   and generously
and to remember that *you*
   gave them to us;
through Jesus Christ our Lord. **Amen.**

21.36   THANKSGIVING FOR THE HARVEST
Jamie Wallace

Thank you, God, for the harvest:

For farmers ploughing and digging, tending and reaping the crops, breeding flocks and herds: God, we give you thanks,
and bring you our praise.

For fishermen, miners and oilmen who live dangerously to feed and warm us: God, we give you thanks,
and bring you our praise.

For businessmen and women, sailors and airmen, and those who drive lorries and trains bringing the food to our shops: God, we give you thanks,
and bring you our praise.

For shopkeepers, check-out staff and roundspeople; for all who cook meals and lay tables and do the washing up: God, we give you thanks,
and bring you our praise.

All this work that people do – and your

→

miraculous gifts of soil and frost, sunshine and rain, and the mystery of growth and ripening!
Forgive us, heavenly Father,
for taking it so much for granted.

Forgive us also for the times we have been selfish with the things that you have given.
Help us to see the wonder of it all;
show us how to help hungry people
to have their fair share
for Jesus' sake. Amen.

21.37   THANKSGIVING
          FOR THE HARVEST
Dick Williams, adapted

Lord of all creation, we gratefully acknowledge our dependence on you for all the good things we enjoy.

For the fruits of the earth, O Lord:
we give you thanks and praise.

For the harvest of the sea, O Lord:
we give you thanks and praise.

For the wealth of the mines, O Lord:
we give you thanks and praise.

For all the beauty of the world in which we live, O Lord:
we give you thanks and praise.

Accept our thanksgiving,
and fill our hearts with praise;
through Jesus Christ our Lord. Amen.

21.38   WE GIVE THANKS FOR
          GOD'S PROVISION
Frank Colquhoun, adapted

Almighty God, we are taught by you that for our daily needs we are dependent not only on the work of our hands but also on your providence and care.

For your gifts to us in nature by which the earth is enriched and made fruitful:

with thankful hearts,
we praise and adore you.

For the labours of those by whom the harvest is gathered in: with thankful hearts,
we praise and adore you.

For all that we receive at your hands: with thankful hearts,
we praise and adore you.

O God, teach us
that in the whole of life
we are workers together with you,
the author and giver of all good things;
through Jesus Christ our Lord. Amen.

21.39   FOR GRATEFUL HEARTS
From 'New Every Morning'

Heavenly Father, giver of all things:
make us more thankful
    for what we have received,
make us more content
    with what we have,
make us more mindful of people in need,
and make us more ready to help
    and serve them
in whatever way we can,
as servants of Jesus Christ our Lord.
Amen.

21.40   ABOUT OUR POSSESSIONS
Michael Botting

Lord Jesus Christ,
you have taught us
that we cannot love
    both God and money,
and that all our possessions
are a trust from you:
teach us to be faithful stewards
of our time, our talents, and our money,
that we may help others
    extend your kingdom;
for your name's sake. **Amen.**

22.1 GREETING
From Revelation 1†

Grace and peace to you from Jesus Christ, who is the faithful witness, the firstborn from the dead. **Amen.**

22.6 RESPONSE
From 1 Peter 5†

The God of all grace who calls you in Christ will himself make you strong, firm, and steadfast:
to him be the power for ever and ever. Amen.

22.7 RESPONSE
From Revelation 7†

Salvation belongs to our God, who sits on the throne, and to the Lamb:
Amen!

**Praise and glory
and wisdom and thanks and honour
and power and strength
be to our God for ever and ever. Amen.**

22.9 PRAISE
From Psalm 117†

Praise the Lord, all you nations;
extol him all you peoples!

For his love protecting us is strong;
his faithfulness endures for ever!

22.10 PRAISE
Psalm 117. 1–2†

Praise the Lord, all you nations:
praise him, all you people!

Great is his love towards us:
his faithfulness shall last for ever.

Praise the Lord:
Amen.

22.11 CONFESSION
Guy King

**Heavenly Father,
we are here to worship you,
but first we ask you
to forgive us all our sins:
so many wrong things
    we ought not to have done,
we have done;
so many right things
    we ought to have done
we have not done.
In your mercy forgive us –
help us to do right,
and to reject what is wrong;
through Jesus Christ our Lord. Amen.**

22.12 CONFESSION
Editors

**Father, we are truly sorry
    for causing you grief
and we repent.
Please forgive us
and cast away all shadows of guilt.
Cleanse us, release us,
bless us, refresh us.
And bring us once again
    into your glorious light,
so that we may receive your comfort
and rejoice in your love;
through Jesus our redeemer. Amen.**

22.14 COLLECT
Pentecost 9, ASB 1980

Almighty God,
you call us to your service:
give us strength to put on the armour
    you provide
that we may resist the assaults
    of the devil,
and ever trust in the salvation
which you have promised us
in Jesus Christ our Lord. **Amen.**

22.15 PSALM
Psalm 46.1–11†

The congregation may divide at A and B; V can be a distant voice, or said by the minister

God is our refuge and strength:
an ever-present help in trouble.

Therefore we will not fear:
A **though the earth should shake,**
B **though the mountains fall**
into the sea,
A **though the waters surge and foam,**
B **though the mountains shake**
and roar.

The Lord almighty is with us:
ALL **the God of Jacob is our fortress.**

There is a river whose streams make glad the city of God, the holy place where the Most High dwells.
A **God is within her, she will not fall:**
B **God will help her at break of day.**

Nations are in uproar, kingdoms fall:
A **God lifts his voice –**
B **the earth melts away.**

The Lord Almighty is with us:
ALL **the God of Jacob is our fortress.**

Come and see what God has done:
ALL **his devastation on the earth!**

He stops the wars throughout the world:
A **he breaks the bow**
and shatters the spear –
B **he sets the shield on fire.**

V Be still, and know that I am God: I will be exalted over the nations, I will be exalted over the earth.

The Lord Almighty is with us:
ALL **the God of Jacob is our fortress.**
Amen.

22.16 PSALM
Psalm 66.1–20†

The congregation may divide at A, B, and C

Praise your God with shouts of joy:
all the earth, sing praise to him.

Sing the glory of his name:
A **offer him your highest praise.**

Say to him: How great you are:
B **wonderful the things you do!**

All your enemies bow down:
C **all the earth sings praise to you.**

Come and see what God has done:
A **causing mortal men to fear –**
B **for he turned the sea to land,**
C **let his people safely through.**

We rejoice at what he does –
A **ruling through eternity,**
B **watching over all the world,**
C **keeping every rebel down.**

Praise our God, you nations, praise:
A **let the sound of praise be heard!**
B **God sustains our very lives:**
C **keeps our feet upon the way.**

Once, you tested us, O God –
A **silver purified by fire –**

Let us fall into a trap,
B **placed hard burdens on our backs –**

Sent us through the flame and flood:
C **now you bring us safely home.**

I will come to worship you:
A **bring to you my offering,**
B **give you what I said I would,**
C **when the troubles threatened me.**

All who love and honour God:
A **come and listen, while I tell**
B **what great things he did for me**
C **when I cried to him for help,**
A **when I praised him with my songs.**

B **When my heart was free from sin,**
C **then he listened to my prayer.**

Praise the Lord who heard my cry:
ALL **God has shown his love to me!**
Amen.

22.20 CREED
Hebrews 4.16†

Let us hold firmly to the faith we profess:

We have a great High Priest
who has gone into the very presence
  of God;
one who can feel sympathy
  for our weakness,
who was tempted
in every way that we are
but did not sin –
Jesus, the Son of God.

Let us have confidence and approach
God's throne, where we will receive
mercy and grace to help us when we
need it. **Amen.**

22.21 CREED
From 1 Timothy 3 and 2 Timothy 2†

Let us proclaim the mystery of our faith:

We believe in one Lord Jesus Christ:
he was revealed in the flesh,
attested by the Spirit,
seen by angels,
proclaimed to the nations,
believed in throughout the world,
and taken up to glory. Amen.

If we died with him,
we shall live with him.

If we endure,
we shall reign with him. Amen.

22.22 CREED
From Revelation 1†

We believe in God almighty,
the Lord, the first and the last,
who is, who was and who is to come.

We believe in Jesus Christ,
the faithful witness,
the first to be raised from death,
the ruler of the kings of earth:
he loves us,
and by his sacrificial death
he has freed us from our sins
and made us a kingdom of priests
to serve our God and Father. Amen.

22.38 FOR THOSE IN SCHOOLS
St Michael-le-Belfrey, York

Heavenly Father,
we pray for every boy and girl among us
who goes to school,
and for every adult who is a teacher:
let our schools teach what is true,
and make each one of us
willing to learn;
for Jesus' sake. **Amen.**

22.40 FOR TEACHERS
Liturgical Commision

Bless those who teach,
that they may increase
  our understanding,
and be open to your word for them:

Jesus, Lord of your Church,
in your mercy hear us. Amen.

22.43 FOR OUR HOMES
         AND FAMILIES
St Michael-le-Belfrey, York

Heavenly Father,
we thank you for our homes,
for our food and clothing,
our families and our fellowship,
and for all the happiness
  we share together;
we ask that your love will surround us,
your care protect us,
and that we shall know your peace
  at all times;
for Jesus' sake. **Amen.**

22.49 FOR RIGHT BEHAVIOUR
From Psalm 141†

O Lord, we call to you:
come quickly in answer to our prayer.
We lift our hearts and our hands to you:
set a guard over our mouths,
a sentry at the door of our lips;
keep us from wanting to do wrong
or joining in evil deeds.
Help us to accept correction
given to us in kindness
  from good people.   →

Strengthen us to pray for the wicked,
but to reject their enticing ways;
for the glory of your name. **Amen.**

22.51 FOR HUMILITY
From Psalm 131†

O Lord God,
keep our hearts from pride,
keep our eyes from haughty looks,
keep our minds from arrogance,
keep our spirit calm
    in childlike dependence upon you:
for you are our hope
both now and for evermore. **Amen.**

22.52 AGAINST TEMPTATION
From Psalm 141†

O sovereign Lord,
when the enemy
    seeks to tempt and ensnare us,
fix our eyes on you
that we may pass by in safety:
then yours shall be the glory. **Amen.**

22.54 PRAISE AND ADORATION
Editors

Our God and Father, we rejoice today
and give you thanks for everything in life
that leads to wholeness and fulfilment:

For strength of body, mind and Spirit, for
healing and health, for power to think
and apply knowledge, for craft, design
and art: we praise you –
we give you thanks, our God.

For life's pleasures and creative gifts, for
the uplifting notes of music, for the
expressive words of prose and poetry, for
the satisfaction found in our enjoyment
of gardens and homes: we praise you –
we give you thanks, our God.

For knowledge of all that is true, noble,
right, pure, lovely and honourable,
for moments of grace and spiritual

awakening, for sensitive awareness of
others in need: we praise you –
we give you thanks, our God.

For your living church, the body of
Christ on earth, for the mystery of your
grace which reaches into our sinful lives,
for the wonder of redemption in Jesus
Christ, for the indwelling of the Holy
Spirit, who enables us to live to your
glory: we praise you –
we give you thanks, our God.

**Our God and Father,
hear and accept our
thanksgiving for your love's sake.
Amen.**

22.55 DEDICATION
Editors

Jesus, Son of God,
let your love shine through our eyes,
your Spirit inspire our words,
your wisdom fill our minds,
your mercy control our hands,
your will capture our hearts,
your joy pervade our being;
until we are changed into your likeness
from glory to glory. **Amen.**

22.56 GLORIA
Liturgical Commision

In a world of change and hope,
    of fear and adventure:
faithful God,
glorify your name. **Amen.**

22.67 BLESSING
From 1 Peter 5†

The God of all grace who called you to
his eternal glory in Christ, make you
strong, firm and steadfast:
**to him be the power for ever and ever.
Amen.**

23.1 GREETING

From 2 Corinthians 13†

The God of love and peace be with you.
Amen.

23.11 RESPONSE
From 1 Corinthians 15†

When the perishable has been clothed
with the imperishable, and the mortal
with immortality, then the saying that is
written will come true:
**Death has been swallowed up
    in victory. Amen.**

23.12 RESPONSE
From 1 Corinthians 15†

The sting of death is sin, and the power
of sin is the law!
**But thanks be to God!
He gives us the victory
through our Lord Jesus Christ. Amen.**

23.16 PRAISE
From Psalm 86†

O Lord our God,
we will praise you with all our heart.

O Lord our God,
**we will proclaim your greatness
    for ever.**

Great is your constant love for us;
**you have saved us from the grave itself!
Amen.**

23.17 CONFESSION
Editor

O God, our Father in heaven, we confess
to you our failure to live as children of
your grace and heirs of your promises:

When we make this world's goods our
treasure, and are mindless of your
kingdom and your reward: in your
mercy,
Father, forgive us and help us.

When we forget that here we have no
enduring city, and fail to look for the city
which is to come: in your mercy,
Father, forgive us and help us.

When we measure worth by the
standards of this passing age and reject
your eternal truth: in your mercy,
Father, forgive us and help us.

When we lose the vision of Christ and no
longer run to win the prize of your call to
heaven: in your mercy,
Father, forgive us and help us.

**Father,
you have raised us together with Christ:
set our hearts and minds
on things above,
where he is seated in glory
at your right hand for evermore. Amen.**

23.18 CONFESSION
Editors

Father God, you know just how much we
need your mercy and continuing
forgiveness.

We are caught up with the trivialities and
distractions of life, which blind us to the
essential and eternal issues, in your
mercy,
Lord God, forgive us and help us.

When we see glimpses of your glory and
of the reality of heaven and we do not
allow that vision to transform the way
we live on earth, in your mercy,
Lord God, forgive us and help us.

When we concentrate almost exclusively
on building treasure on earth, and we
become mindless of your kingdom and
careless of our reward, in your mercy,
Lord God, forgive us and help us.

When we lose the vision of Christ, and
fail to strive after the abundant life which
you offer us, in your mercy,
Lord God, forgive us and help us.

→

Father,
you have raised us together with Christ:
set our hearts and minds
on things above
where he is seated in glory
at your right hand for evermore. Amen.

23.19 CONFESSION
From Psalm 109†

O Lord, we need you:
our hearts are wounded,
our days fade like evening shadows,
we are weak and despise ourselves;
for we have sinned against you.
Forgive us, O Lord,
and in your constant love save us;
through Jesus our redeemer. Amen.

23.21 COLLECT
Last Sunday after Pentecost, ASB 1980

Merciful God,
you have prepared
   for those who love you
such good things
   as pass our understanding.
Pour into our hearts
such love towards you
that we, loving you above all things,
may obtain your promises,
which exceed all that we can desire;
through Jesus Christ our Lord. **Amen.**

23.22 COLLECT
Funeral Service, ASB 1980

Heavenly Father,
in your Son Jesus Christ
you have given us a true faith
and a sure hope.
Strengthen this faith and hope in us
all our days,
that we may live as those who believe
in the communion of saints,
the forgiveness of sins,
and the resurrection to eternal life;
through your Son Jesus Christ our Lord.
Amen.

23.23 PSALM
Psalm 33.1–22†

The congregation – and ministers – may
divide at A and B

Sing joyfully to the Lord, you
righteous:
it is right
that his people should praise him.

Praise the Lord with the harp:
A **make music to him on the strings.**

Sing to the Lord a new song:
B **play skilfully, and shout for joy.**

For the word of the Lord is right and
true:
ALL **and all his work is faithfulness.**

The Lord loves righteousness and
justice:
A **his endless love fills the earth.**

By the word of the Lord the skies
were formed:
B **his breath created moon and stars.**

Let all the earth fear the Lord:
ALL **the people of the world revere him.**

For he spoke, and it came to be:
A **he commanded, and all was made.**

The Lord holds back the nations:
B **he thwarts their evil intent.**

God's purposes are sure:
ALL **his plans endure for ever.**

Happy is the nation whose God is
the Lord:
A **happy the people**
   he makes his own.

The eyes of the Lord are on those
who fear him:
B **who trust in his unfailing love.**

We wait in hope for the Lord:
A **he is our help and shield.**

In him our hearts rejoice:
B **we trust his holy name.**

May your constant love be with us,
Lord:
ALL **as we put our hope in you. Amen.**

23.26 CREED
From 2 Corinthians, 4 and 5†

We speak because we believe:

God,
who raised the Lord Jesus Christ to life,
will also raise us up with Jesus
and take us together into his presence.

Though outwardly we are
wasting away,
inwardly we are being renewed
day by day;
we live by faith, and not by sight.
Amen.

23.27 CREED
From Revelation 2†

We believe in Jesus Christ
before whom we fall down and worship
but need not be afraid:
he is the first and the last,
the living one;
he has authority over death
and the world of the dead,
for he was dead, but now is alive
for ever and ever. Amen.

23.28 CREED
From 2 Thessalonians 2 and 3†

Let us affirm the teaching to which we
hold:

We believe in God the Father
who loved us,
and by his grace gave us
eternal encouragement and good hope.

We believe in God the Son
who encourages our hearts
and strengthens us
  in every good deed and word;
whose grace shall be with us all.

We believe in God the Holy Spirit,
the Lord of peace
who gives us peace at all times
and in every way.

We believe in one God:
Father, Son and Holy Spirit. Amen.

23.32 FOR THE BROKEN-HEARTED
Editors

The Lord is near to the broken-hearted
and saves the crushed in spirit. *(Psalm 34)*

Let us pray for broken homes, for
teenagers torn by doubts and
disillusionment, for old people
bewildered by infirmities and lack of
contact, for sick people fearful of the
future, and for those who mourn:

O God our redeemer,
on behalf of all people in distress,
especially those known to us,
we claim your promise
to be near the broken-hearted,
and to save the crushed in spirit:
use us as channels
  of your healing power;
through Jesus Christ our Lord. Amen.

23.42 IN TROUBLE OR DIFFICULTY
From 'New Every Morning'

Father, give to us, and to all your people,
in times of anxiety, serenity;
in times of hardship, courage;
in times of uncertainty, patience;
and, at all times,
a quiet trust in your wisdom and love;
through Jesus Christ our Lord. **Amen.**

23.46 FOR STRENGTH
AND SERENITY
From 2 Thessalonians 2†

O God our Father,
you loved us
and by your grace gave us
eternal courage and good hope:
encourage our hearts
and strengthen us
in every good deed and word;
let the Spirit of peace give us peace
at all times
and in every way;
and may the grace
  of the Lord Jesus Christ
be with us all. **Amen.**

23.47   FOR JESUS TO BE NEAR US
Editors

Lord Jesus,
when the unexpected happens
and we feel lost or afraid,
help us to remember that
   your peace is our comfort,
   your love is our strength,
   your presence is our joy.
Thank you, Lord for your light
when the way is dark. **Amen.**

23.48   FOR INWARD PEACE
Christina Rossetti

O Lord, your way is perfect:
help us, we pray,
always to trust in your goodness;
that walking with you in faith,
and following you in all simplicity,
we may possess
   quiet and contented minds,
and leave all our worries with you,
because you care for us;
for the sake of Jesus Christ our Lord.
Amen.

23.52   FOR FAITH
David Silk

Grant to us, Lord God,
to trust you
not for ourselves alone,
but for those also whom we love
and who are hidden from us
by the shadow of death;
that, as we believe your power
to have raised
our Lord Jesus Christ
   from the dead,
so we may trust your love
to give eternal life
to all who believe in him;
through Jesus Christ our Lord,
who is alive
and reigns with you and the Holy Spirit,
one God, now and for ever. **Amen.**

23.59   THANKSGIVING
St Boniface, adapted

O God,
we cannot measure your love,
nor ever count your blessings:
we thank you for all your goodness;
for in our weakness you make us strong,
in our darkness you give us light,
and in our sorrows
   you bring comfort and peace.
And from everlasting to everlasting
you are our God,
Father, Son, and Holy Spirit. **Amen.**

23.61   FOR GOD'S HELP IN ALL
         CIRCUMSTANCES
From 'A New Zealand Prayer Book'

In darkness and in light,
in trouble and in joy,
help us, heavenly Father,
to trust your love,
to serve your purpose,
and to praise your name,
through Jesus Christ our Lord. **Amen.**

23.62   ASCRIPTION
From Philippians 4†

O God, let your peace
which passes all understanding,
keep our hearts and minds
   in Christ Jesus;
and to you be glory
for ever and ever. **Amen.**

23.63   ASCRIPTION
Martin Luther King

And now to him who is able
   to keep us from falling,
and lift us from the dark valley of despair
to the bright mountain of hope,
from the midnight of desperation
to the daybreak of joy;
to him be power and authority,
   for ever and ever. **Amen.**

23.66 DEDICATION
Roger Pickering

And now, O Father in heaven,
we entrust ourselves to you;
that joyful or sorrowing,
living or dying,
we may ever be with our Lord Jesus,
safe in your eternal care. **Amen.**

23.65 DEDICATION
Elizabeth Goudge

Eternal Light, shine in our hearts,
eternal Goodness, deliver us from evil,
eternal Power, be our support,
eternal Wisdom, scatter our darkness,
eternal Pity, have mercy upon us:
that with all our heart and mind
    and soul and strength
we may seek your face,
and be brought by your infinite mercy
to your holy presence;
through Jesus Christ our Lord. **Amen.**

Christ's Coming, Judgement

24.1 GREETING
From Revelation 1†

Grace and peace to you from him who is,
and who was, and who is to come.
Amen.

THE ADVENT WREATH
Jane Austin

24.2 ADVENT 1 – THE PATRIARCHS
Genesis 12.2,3; Genesis 26.24; Deuteronomy 18.15; 2 Samuel 23.3

As we light the candles in our Advent
Wreath we remember the preparations
which God our Father made for the
coming of his Son into the world.

Today is the First Sunday in Advent: we
remember how God spoke to Abraham,
Isaac, Moses and David and told them of
the Messiah who was to come.

Abraham was promised, that through his
descendants all the world world be
blessed.
Thank you, Father.

Isaac was told, 'Do not be afraid, for I am
with you.'
Thank you, Father.

Moses looked forward to the One who
would be raised up to take his place as
the leader of the people.
Thank you, Father.

David knew that a king would follow
him who would reign for ever.
Thank you, Father.

The first candle is lit (the centre candle remaining unlit until Christmas Day)

As we light this first candle we
remember Abraham, Isaac, Moses and
David and, like them, we look forward to
the coming Messiah. **Amen.**

24.3 ADVENT 2 – THE PROPHETS
Isaiah 9.6; Jeremiah 3.15; Ezekiel 20.41; Micah 5.2.

The previous Sunday's candle is lit.

As we light the candles in our Advent
Wreath we remember the preparations
which God our Father made for the
coming of his Son into the world. Our
first candle reminds us of Abraham,
Isaac, Moses and David who looked
forward to the coming of Jesus.

Today is the Second Sunday in Advent:
we remember how God our Father

→

also spoke to people through his prophets and told *them* of the Christ who was to come.

Isaiah said, 'A child is born to us! A son is given to us! He will be called Wonderful Counsellor, Mighty God, Eternal Father, Prince of Peace.'
Praise you, Lord.

Jeremiah said, '"The Days are coming," says the Lord, "when I will choose as king a righteous descendant of David. This king will reign wisely and do what is just and right in the land. This is the name by which he will be called: The Lord our Salvation."'
Praise you, Lord.

Ezekiel said, 'I will show myself holy among you in the sight of the nations. Then you will know that I am the Lord.'
Praise you, Lord

Micah said, 'Out of Bethlehem will come for me one who will be ruler over Israel, whose origins are from of old, from ancient times.'
Praise you, Lord.

The second candle is lit

As we light this second candle we remember Isaiah, Jeremiah, Ezekiel and Micah, who prepared the way for the Messiah who was to come. **Amen.**

24.4   ADVENT 3 – THE FORERUNNER
John 1.29; John 1.34; Luke 3.16; Mark 1.10,11

The previous Sunday's two candles are lit

As we light the candles in our Advent Wreath we remember the preparations which God our Father made for the coming of his Son into the world. Our first candle reminds us of Abraham, Isaac, Moses and David who looked forward to the coming of Jesus. Our second candle reminds us of Isaiah, Jeremiah, Ezekiel and Micah who told of the coming Messiah.

Today is the Third Sunday in Advent: we remember how John the Baptist was sent to prepare the way for the Lord.

John testified, 'Look, the Lamb of God who takes away the sin of the world!'
Praise you, Lord.

John said, 'I have seen and I testify that this is the Son of God.'
Praise you, Lord.

John promised, 'He will baptise you with the Holy Spirit and with fire.'
Praise you, Lord.

John saw the Holy Spirit descend on Jesus like a dove. And a voice came from heaven, 'You are my Son, whom I love; with you I am well pleased.'
Praise you, Lord.

The third candle is lit.

We light this third candle and remember John the Baptist, who came to prepare the way for the Lord. **Amen.**

24.5   ADVENT 4 –
            THE VIRGIN MARY
Luke 1.30; Luke 1.35; Luke 1.49; Matthew 1.23

The previous Sunday's three candles are lit

As we light the candles in our Advent Wreath we remember the preparations which God our Father made for the coming of his Son into the world. Our first candle reminds us of Abraham, Isaac, Moses and David who looked forward to the coming of Jesus. Our second candle reminds us of Isaiah, Jeremiah, Ezekiel and Micah who told of the coming Messiah. Our third candle reminds us of John the Baptist who came to prepare the way for the Lord.

Today is the Fourth Sunday in Advent: we remember how Jesus, the Son of God was born of a human mother so that he was truly both God and man.

The angel Gabriel said, 'Do not be afraid, Mary, you have found favour with God.'
Thank you, Father.

Gabriel said to Mary, 'The holy one to be born of you will be called the Son of God.'
Thank you, Father.

Mary said, 'The Mighty One has done great things for me – holy is his name.'
Thank you, Father.

They will call him Immanuel, which means, God with us.
Thank you, Father.

The fourth candle is lit

As we light this fourth candle, we remember Mary who was obedient and so became the mother of Jesus. **Amen.**

24.6 CHRISTMAS DAY – CHRIST THE LIGHT OF THE WORLD

All the Advent Sunday candles are lit, leaving the one in the centre

As we light the candles in our Advent Wreath we remember the preparations which God our Father made for the coming of his Son into the world. Our first candle reminds us of Abraham, Isaac, Moses and David who looked forward to the coming of Jesus. Our second candle reminds us of Isaiah, Jeremiah, Ezekiel and Micah who told of the coming Messiah. Our third candle reminds us of John the Baptist who came to prepare the way for the Lord. Our fourth candle reminds us of Mary who was obedient and became the mother of Jesus.

The centre candle is lit.

Today is Christmas Day: on this special day we light the last candle and rejoice together:
Christ, the Light of the World has come! Amen.

24.18 RESPONSE
From Romans 13†

Now is the time to wake from sleep:
our salvation is nearer than when we first believed.

24.19 RESPONSE
From Isaiah 40†

The glory of the Lord shall be revealed:
and everyone shall see it together!

24.20 RESPONSE
From Daniel 4†

We tell of the miraculous signs and wonders that the Most High God has performed for us:

How great are his signs:
how mighty are his wonders!

His kingdom is eternal:
his reign endures from generation to generation for ever! Amen.

24.21 RESPONSE
From Revelation 1†

Look, he is coming with the clouds:
and every eye will see him. Even those who pierced him.

All the peoples of the earth shall mourn because of him.
So shall it be! Amen.

24.22 RESPONSE
From Revelation 1†

Look, he is coming on the clouds:
everyone will see him.

All people on earth will mourn over him:
so shall it be!

'I am the first and the last,' says the Lord God Almighty:
who is, who was, and who is to come. Amen.

24.23 RESPONSE
From Revelation 11†

The kingdom of this world has become
the kingdom of our Lord and of his
Christ:
he will reign for ever and ever. Amen.

24.25 PRAISE
From Psalms 82 and 83†

Come, O God, and rule the earth:
every land belongs to you.

Let them know that you are king,
sovereign over all the world! Amen.

24.26 CONFESSION
Editors

We must give account of our
stewardship: let us ask forgiveness for
our sin and failure.

Lord, we have not used your gifts wisely:
forgive us for being unprofitable; in your
mercy,
hear us and help us.

Lord, we have not kept brightly burning
the light you entrusted to us: forgive us
for being unprepared; in your mercy,
hear us and help us.

Lord, we have sometimes ended the day
in anger or bitterness: forgive us for
being unrepentant: in your mercy,
hear us and help us.

Renew our vision,
restore our watchfulness,
make us faithful as you are faithful,
that when you come in glory
we may hear you say:
'Enter into the joy of your Lord.' Amen.

24.27 CONFESSION
Liturgical Commision

Lord God, we come to you
with sorrow for our sins;
and we ask for your help and strength.
Help us to know ourselves
and to accept our weakness.

Strengthen us with your forgiving love,
so that we may more courageously
  follow and obey your Son,
whose birth we are soon to celebrate.
Amen.

24.28 CONFESSION
From Psalm 51†

O God, in your goodness have mercy on
us, wash us clean from our guilt:
and purify us from our sin.

We know our faults well:
and our sins hang heavy upon us.

Against you only have we sinned:
and done evil in your sight.

So you are right to judge us:
you are justified in condemning us.

Remove our sin and we will be clean:
wash us,
and we will be whiter than snow.

Hide your face from our sins:
and wipe out all our guilt
through Jesus Christ our Lord. Amen.

24.29 CONFESSION
From Nehemiah 9†

O our God,
the great, mighty and awesome God,
gracious and merciful;
you keep your covenant of love –
you have acted faithfully
  while we have done wrong.
We did not follow your commandment
or pay attention
to the warnings you gave us;
even while we were enjoying
  your great goodness
we did not serve you,
or turn from our evil ways;
because of our sin
our happiness is taken away –
our enemy rules even our souls
  and bodies
and we are in great distress.
Forgive us and restore us
  for your name's sake. Amen.

24.31 COLLECT
Advent, ASB 1980

Almighty God,
give us grace
to cast away the works of darkness
and to put on the armour of light,
now in the time of this mortal life,
in which your Son Jesus Christ
   came to us in great humility:
so that on the last day,
when he shall come again
   in his glorious majesty
to judge the living and the dead,
we may rise to the life immortal;
through him who is alive and reigns
   with you and the Holy Spirit,
one God, now and for ever. **Amen.**

24.32 PSALM
Psalm 98.1–9†

The congregation may divide at A and B

O sing to the Lord a new song:
for he has done marvellous things.

His right hand and his holy arm:
have brought a great triumph to us.

He lets his salvation be known:
A **his righteousness seen
by the world.**

His glory is witnessed by all.
B **To us he continues his love:**

Rejoice in the Lord, all the earth:
ALL **and burst into jubilant song.**

Make music to God with the harp:
A **with songs
and the sound of your praise.**

With trumpets and blast of the horn:
B **sing praises to God as your king.**

Let rivers and streams clap their
hands:
A **the mountains together sing praise.**

The Lord comes to judge the whole
earth:
B **in righteousness
God rules the world.**

All **Amen.**

24.34 CREED
From Colossians 1

**God has rescued us
from the power of darkness,
   and brought us safe
into the kingdom of his dear Son:
in Christ our sins are forgiven,
we are set free. Amen.**

24.35 CREED
Holy Communion, ASB 1980

Let us proclaim the mystery of our faith:
**Christ has died,
Christ is risen,
Christ will come again.**

24.36 CREED
From Revelation 4 and 5†

We say together in faith:
**Holy, holy, holy
is the Lord God Almighty,
who was, and is, and is to come.**

We believe in God the Father, who
created all things:
**for by his will they were created
and have their being.**

We believe in God the Son, who was
slain:
**for with his blood,
he purchased us for God,
from every tribe and language
and people and nation.**

We believe in God the Holy Spirit—
**the Spirit and the Bride say, 'Come!'
Even so, come, Lord Jesus! Amen.**

24.42 ABOUT THE END OF TIME
From Mark 13†

When the skies grow dark and buildings
fall, then hear us, Lord:
have mercy on us.

When the deceivers come and the nations
rise in anger, then hear us, Lord:
have mercy on us.

When the famines begin, and when the

earth shakes to bring the future to birth,
then hear us, Lord:
have mercy on us.

When we stand for a witness, when we
are arrested and betrayed, then hear us,
Lord:
have mercy on us.

When the sun is darkened and the moon
fails to give us light, and the stars fall
from the sky, then hear us, Lord:
have mercy on us.

When you come in your great power and
glory with your angels from heaven;
have mercy, Lord:
gather us from the four winds
from the ends of the earth
to be with you for ever. Amen.

24.43   ACT OF PRAISE
          (AT HOLY COMMUNION)
St Catherine's, Houghton-on-the-Hill,
Leicester

Jesus, you came to live among us, born of
the virgin Mary. We give you thanks:
and praise your holy name.

Jesus, you come to us as we read your
story in the Bible. We give you thanks:
and praise your holy name.

Jesus, you come to us as we take in faith
the bread and wine. We give you thanks:
and praise your holy name.

Jesus, you will come to reign in glory. We
give you thanks:
and praise your holy name.

Amen. Come, Lord Jesus!

24.44   THANKSGIVING
Editors

Our gracious God, out of chaos and
darkness in the beginning you brought
into being the splendour of the universe
and the world in all its beauty. God, we
praise you:
God, we thank you.

At the right time you sent your Son to be
the light of the world, to lead us out of
spiritual darkness into the marvellous
brightness of your truth. In him has
dawned the day of resurrection life. God,
we praise you:
God, we thank you.

Above all the noise and movement of
this world today, we look for the coming
of the new heaven and earth, 'the holy
city of God'. Lord Jesus, you are coming
again in great power and glory. God, we
praise you:
God, we thank you.

We thank you that you are in this world,
by your Spirit preparing a people for this
next great cosmic event. God, we praise
you:
God, we thank you.

We thank you that you are healing lives
that have been torn and broken by sin,
and that you are filling us with joy and
hope. God, we praise you:
God, we thank you.

Lord God, we await the dawning of the
new day when the earth shall be filled
with the glory of God as the waters cover
the sea.
To God be praise and thanks
for evermore. Amen.

24.45   DEDICATION: A PERSONAL
          PRAYER
Editors

Call me, infant Lord Jesus;
draw me to the stable
   where your cradle was a manger,
let me kneel before you,
   God's own Lamb,
and worship you.

Call me, crucified Christ;
draw me to the Cross
   where you suffered
   and yet still prayed,
let me kneel before your act of pure love
and worship you.

Call me, Prince of Life;
draw me to your side
   for you are risen and here among us,
let me kneel before the light of your
   holiness
and worship you,
and pledge myself anew. **Amen.**

24.46 INVOCATION (ADVENT)
From 'The Promise of His Glory'

Come, Lord Jesus, do not delay;
give new courage to your people
who trust in your love.
By your coming
raise us to the joy of your kingdom,
where you live and reign,
with the Father and the Spirit,
one God for ever and ever. **Amen.**

24.47 INVOCATION
        (BEFORE CHRISTMAS)
Editor

Jesus, who came to earth
  as a helpless baby;
Jesus, the Lamb of God born in a stable;
Jesus, the Prince of Peace
  who slept on hay;
Jesus, whose birth caused
  the angels to sing;
Jesus, whose glory lit up the sky;
Jesus, whose coming was foretold;
Jesus, who gave us his life;
Jesus, who draws us with love;
Jesus, our saviour, our king:
come, Lord Jesus, come. Amen.

God's Word to Us, Proclamation

25.1 GREETING
From 2 Peter 1†

Grace and peace be yours in full measure
through the knowledge of God and of
Jesus our Lord. **Amen.**

25.9 RESPONSE
From 2 Samuel 22†

You are our lamp, O Lord:
turn our darkness into light. Amen.

25.10 RESPONSE
From 2 Timothy 3 and Psalm 119†

All Scripture is inspired by God, and is
useful for teaching the truth, rebuking
error, correcting faults, and giving
instruction for right living:
**your word is a lamp to my feet
and a light for my path. Amen.**

25.11 RESPONSE
From Hebrews 5†

Anyone who has to drink milk is still a
baby; solid food is for grown people: let
us go forward, then, to mature teaching.
Let us go forward:
this we will do, God helping us. Amen.

25.12 RESPONSE
From Jeremiah 15†

Your words are our joy and our heart's
delight:
**for we bear your name,
O Lord God almighty. Amen.**

25.15 PRAISE
From Psalm 67†

Let the people praise you, O God;
let all the people praise you!

Let your ways be known on earth;
**your saving power in all the world!
Amen.**

25.16 CONFESSION
From 2 Kings 22†

**Lord, we have not obeyed your word,
nor heeded
    what is written in the Scriptures:
we repent with all our heart,
and humble ourselves before you.
In your mercy forgive us:
grant us your peace
and the strength to keep your laws;
through Jesus Christ our Lord. Amen.**

25.17 CONFESSION
From Psalm 119†

**Lord, we are to blame,
for we have not followed your law,
we have not kept your commandments,
we have not sought for you
    with all our heart,
we have not walked in your ways,
nor have we fully obeyed you;
Lord, we long to be faithful
    and obedient:
do not put us to shame.
Give us upright hearts,
teach us obedience
and do not forsake us for ever. Amen.**

25.19 COLLECT
A Prayer of Dedication, ASB 1980

Almighty God,
we thank you for the gift
    of your holy word.
Let it be a lantern to our feet,
a light to our paths,
and a strength to our lives.
Take us and use us
to love and serve
in the power of the Holy Spirit
and in the name of your Son,
Jesus Christ our Lord. **Amen.**

25.20 PSALM
Psalm 111.1–10†

The congregation may divide at A and B

Praise the Lord:
praise the Lord!

With my whole heart I will thank the
Lord: in the company of his people.
Great are the works of the Lord:
A **those who wonder, seek them.**

Glorious and majestic are his deeds:
B **his goodness lasts for ever.**

He reminds us of his works of grace:
A **he is merciful and kind.**

He sustains those who fear him:
B **he keeps his covenant always.**

All he does is right and just:
A **all his words are faithful.**

They will last for ever and ever:
B **and be kept in faith and truth.**

He provided redemption for his
people, and made an eternal
covenant with them:
ALL **holy and awesome is his name!**

The fear of the Lord is the beginning
of wisdom; he gives understanding
to those who obey:
ALL **to God belongs eternal praise!
Amen.**

25.21 PSALM
Psalm 149.1–9†

*The congregation – and ministers – may
divide at A and B*

Praise the Lord:
praise the Lord!

Sing a new song to the Lord:
A **let the people shout his name!**

Praise your maker, Israel:
B **hail your king, Jerusalem.**

Sing and dance to honour him:
A **praise him with the strings
and drums.**

God takes pleasure in his saints:
B **crowns the meek with victory.**

Rise, you saints, in triumph now:
A **sing the joyful night away!**

Shout aloud and praise your God!
B **Hold aloft the two-edged sword!**

Let the judgement now begin:
A **kings shall fall and tyrants die.**

Through his people, by his word:
B **God shall have the victory!**

Praise the Lord:
ALL **praise the Lord! Amen.**

25.24 RESPONSE
(AFTER A READING)
From Revelation 1–7†

If you have ears to hear, then listen to what the Spirit says to the churches! **Amen.**

25.25 CREED
From Romans 1†

We believe in the Gospel,
promised by God long ago
   through the prophets,
written in the Holy Scriptures.

We believe in God's Son,
   our Lord Jesus Christ:
as to his humanity,
born a descendant of David;
as to his divinity,
shown with great power
   to be the Son of God
by his raising from death. Amen.

25.26 CREED
From 1 Timothy 3†

Let us proclaim the mystery of our faith:

We believe in one Lord Jesus Christ –
he was revealed in the flesh,
attested by the Spirit,
seen by apostles,
proclaimed to the nations,
believed in throughout the world,
and taken up to glory. Amen.

25.27 THANKSGIVING
FOR INSPIRATION
Dick Williams

Thank you, Lord, for the Bible:

For its ability to give us each day new vision and new power: O Lord of inspiration,
we give you thanks and praise.

For its capacity to enter into our minds and spirits, refreshing them and fashioning them anew: O Lord of inspiration,
we give you thanks and praise.

For its power to bring faith to birth and to sustain it: O Lord of inspiration,
we give you thanks and praise.

Thank you, Lord, for the Bible,
through Jesus Christ our Saviour.
Amen.

25.28 THANKSGIVING
FOR GOD'S WORD
Emmanuel Church, Northwood.

Let us thank God for all his blessings:

For your creative word, by which the earth and sky were made: we thank you, Father,
and praise your holy name.

For making us in your own image, able to hear and answer your call: we thank you, Father,
and praise your holy name.

For revealing yourself to people through the ages, and changing their lives: we thank you, Father,
and praise your holy name.

For your word to us in these days, calling us to repentance and assuring us of forgiveness: we thank you, Father,
and praise your holy name.

For promising to hear our prayers, and faithfully meeting our every need: we thank you, Father,
and praise your holy name.

→

Grant that we may worship you,
not only with our voices,
but in true and willing service,
through Jesus Christ our Lord. Amen.

25.29 THANKSGIVING
          FOR THE BIBLE
J Meirion Lloyd, adapted

Let us give thanks to God:

For the majesty of the Law, for the power
of the Prophets, for the wisdom of the
Proverbs and the beauty of the Psalms,
and above all for the grace of the Gospel,
we lift up our hearts in praise:
thanks be to God!

For the Bible in our own language, for
those who long ago gave us translations,
for those who down the years improved
them, enabling the Scriptures to
penetrate deeply into our national life,
we lift up our hearts in praise:
thanks be to God!

For the continuing work of revision to
match our changing language, for all that
the Bible means to Christians throughout
the world, we lift up our hearts in praise:
thanks be to God!

For those who interpret, publish and
distribute the Scriptures in every tongue,
so that all peoples may come to the
knowledge of salvation, we lift up our
hearts in praise:
thanks be to God!

To you, O gracious Father,
with the living Word,
through the one eternal Spirit,
be glory now and for ever. Amen

25.41 THAT WE MAY
          HEAR GOD'S VOICE
Editors

O Lord, voices surround us, always
clamouring, directing, imploring,
accusing; and our own voices are too
strident. May we be quiet and listen, so
that you may speak –

In miracle; in the wonders of human
courage and hope and endurance and
sacrifice that we meet in ordinary people.
O Lord, speak to us:
help us to listen.

In Spirit; in the mysteries beyond our
comprehension, in the faith that defies all
mortal order, in the resurrection truth. O
Lord, speak to us:
help us to listen.

In joy; in laughter, in human warmth, in
triumph over pain, in the experience of
beauty. O Lord, speak to us:
help us to listen.

Speak, O Lord, that we may listen
and tell what great things
   you have done for us,
in Jesus' name. Amen.

25.43 FOR UNDERSTANDING
Michael Botting

Heavenly Father,
you have shown
the wonder of your love for us
   in Jesus Christ
through the Bible:
help us to understand it with our minds,
and apply it in our lives:
for his name's sake. **Amen.**

25.44 FOR STRENGTH
Editors

We pray for God's help as we read his
commands in the Bible, or as we listen to
his word:

When we are tempted to do or say wrong
things, Lord,
speak to us in our selfishness;
help us to be strong.

When we are anxious or afraid, Lord,
speak to us in our fearfulness;
help us to be strong.

When we are ill or in pain, Lord,
speak to us in our helplessness;
help us to be strong.

When things we have to do seem too hard for us, Lord,
**speak to us in our weakness;
help us to be strong.**

**O God,
we will listen to your word;
and by your strength
we will do what you command,
and bring glory to your name. Amen.**

25.46 ABOUT OUR WITNESS
From 'A New Zealand Prayer Book'

Jesus,
new beginning,
heavenly bread,
living water,
we hear the word of life,
we see and grasp the truth:
help us to proclaim it. **Amen.**

25.48 ACT OF PRAISE AND PRAYER
Editors

Lord God, you have spoken to us in the Law of Israel:
we praise and adore you.

You have challenged us in the words of the Prophets:
we praise and adore you.

You have shown us in the Gospel of Jesus what you are really like:
we praise and adore you.

Lord God, because you still come to us now:
we praise and adore you.

You come to us through other people, in their love and concern for us:
thank you, Lord.

You come to us through men and women, young people and children, who need our help:
thank you, Lord.

You come to us as we worship you:
thank you, Lord.

**Lord God, come to us now;
in the power of Jesus Christ. Amen.**

25.50 BLESSING
R. Pynson, adapted

God be in our head,
   and in our understanding;
God be in our eyes, and in our looking;
God be in our mouth,
   and in our speaking;
God be in our heart, and in our thinking;
God be at our end, and at our departing.
Amen.

Christmas

26.1 GREETING
From Titus 1†

Grace and peace to you from God our Father and Jesus Christ our Saviour. **Amen.**

26.9 RESPONSE
From Isaiah 9†

For us a Child is born:
to us a Son is given. Alleluia!

26.10 RESPONSE
From John 1†

The Word became flesh and lived among us:
**we have seen his glory,
the glory of the one and only Son,
who came from the Father,
full of grace and truth.**

26.15 PRAISE
From Psalm 100†

Shout for joy to the Lord, all the earth;
serve the Lord with gladness!

Come before him with joyful songs;
**give thanks to him and praise his name!
Amen.**

26.16 ACT OF PRAISE
From 'Worship Now'

Let us worship the Saviour:

Heavenly king, yet born of Mary; Jesus,
Son of God,
we praise and adore you.

Eternal Word, yet child without speech;
Jesus, Son of God,
we praise and adore you.

Robed in glory, yet wrapped in infant
clothes; Jesus, Son of God,
we praise and adore you.

Lord of heaven and earth, yet laid in a
manger; Jesus, Son of God,
we praise and adore you.

**To you, O Jesus,
strong in your weakness,
glorious in your humility,
mighty to save,
be all praise and glory,
with the Father and the Holy Spirit,
now and for ever. Amen.**

26.17 CONFESSION
John Searle, adapted

We confess that amid all the joys and
festivities of this season we have
sometimes forgotten what Christmas
really means, and have left the Lord Jesus
out of our thinking and living:
Father, forgive us.

Help us to remember that you loved the
world so much that you gave your only
Son, who was born to be our Saviour:
Lord, help us.

We confess that we have allowed the
most important event in history to
become dulled by familiarity:
Father, forgive us.

Help us in this act of worship to
recapture a sense of wonder, and to
discover again the stupendous fact that
the Creator of the universe has come to
us as a newborn baby:
Lord, help us.

We confess to a selfish enjoyment of
Christmas while we do little to help the
homeless families of your world:
Father, forgive us.

**Fill our hearts with the love that cares,
that understands and gives;
show us how we can best serve
     those in need;
for the sake of him
     who was born in a stable,
Jesus Christ our Lord. Amen.**

26.18 CONFESSION
Editors

For our repeated failures to respond to
your boundless generosity, in your
mercy:
Lord, forgive us.

For our aggressive attitudes which sour
human relationships, in your mercy:
Lord, forgive us.

For our self-centredness and lack of love
to the less fortunate who struggle in life,
in your mercy:
Lord, forgive us.

For our placid contentment in a world of
so much hurting and pain, in your mercy:
Lord, forgive us.

**Give us more and more
your strenthening Spirit
as we open our lives to you;
Help us to fulfil your law of love,
now and always. Amen.**

26.19 CONFESSION
From 'A New Zealand Prayer Book'

God of mercy,
we are sorry
that we have not always done
what you wanted us to do.
We have not loved you
  with all our heart,
and we have not cared enough
  for other people.
Forgive us, for Jesus' sake. Amen.

26.20 CONFESSION
From Job 40–42†

Lord, you are without equal;
everything under heaven is yours:
we are unworthy
and have to answer to you.
We confess our lack of understanding
and repent of all our sin.
Lord, our ears have heard of you,
and now our eyes have seen you
in Jesus our Redeemer. Amen.

26.22 COLLECT
David Silk

Holy Jesus
to deliver us from the power of darkness
you humbled yourself
  to be born among us
and laid in a manger.
Let the light of your love
  always shine in our hearts,
and bring us at last
to the joyful vision of your beauty;
for you are now alive
and reign
with the Father and the Holy Spirit,
God for ever and ever. **Amen.**

26.23 PSALM
Psalm 113 1–8

The ministers/leaders may divide at A and B

A Praise the Lord:
  praise the Lord!

B You servants of the Lord, praise his
  name:
  let the name of the Lord be praised,
  both now and for evermore!

A From the rising of the sun to the
  place where it sets:
  the name of the Lord be praised!

B The Lord is exalted above the earth:
  his glory over the heavens.

A Who is like the Lord our God?
  He is throned in the heights above

B Yet he bends down:
  yet he stoops to look at our world.

A He raises the poor from the dust:
  and lifts the needy
  from their sorrow.

BOTH Praise the Lord:
  Amen.

26.24 CANTICLE
From Hebrews 1†

Let us worship the Son of God:

Your throne, O God, will last for ever
and ever:
righteousness
will be the sceptre of your kingdom.

You have loved righteousness and hated
wickedness:
therefore God, your God,
has set you above your companions
by anointing you with the oil of joy.

In the beginning, O Lord, you laid the
foundations of the earth:
and the heavens
are the work of your hands.

They will perish, but you remain:
they will all wear out like clothing.

But you remain the same:
your years will never end. Amen.

26.24 READING: JESUS IS BORN
From Luke 2.8–20, 'The Dramatised Bible'

Narrator
There were shepherds living out in the fields near Bethlehem, keeping watch over their flocks at night. An angel of the Lord appeared to them, and the glory of the Lord shone around them, and they were terrified. But the angel said to them:

Angel
Do not be afraid. I bring you good news of great joy that will be for all the people. Today in the town of David a Saviour has been born to you; he is Christ the Lord. This will be a sign to you: You will find a baby wrapped in cloths and lying in a manger.

Narrator
Suddenly a great company of the heavenly host appeared with the angel, praising God.

Chorus *(joyfully)*
**Glory to God in the highest
and on earth peace
to all on whom his favour rests.**

Narrator
When the angels had left them and gone into heaven, the shepherds said to one another:

Shepherd 1
Let's go to Bethlehem

Shepherd 2
and see this thing that has happened

Shepherd 3
which the Lord has told us about.

Narrator
So they hurried off and found Mary and Joseph, and the baby, who was lying in the manger. When they had seen him, they spread the word concerning what had been told them about this child, and all who heard it were amazed at what the shepherds said to them. (PAUSE) But Mary treasured up all these things and pondered them in her heart. The shepherds returned, glorifying and praising God for all the things they had heard and seen, which were just as they had been told.

Cast
This is the word of the Lord/This is the Gospel of Christ.

People
**Thanks be to God/Praise to Christ
our Lord.**

26.26 CREED
From Hebrews 1†

Let us declare our faith in the Son of God:

**In the past God spoke to our ancestors
through the prophets
at many times and in various ways,
but in these last days
he has spoken to us by his Son,
whom he appointed heir of all things,
and through whom he made the worlds.**

**The Son is the radiance of God's glory,
the exact representation of his being
who sustains all things
by his powerful word.
After he had provided
purification for sins
he sat down at the right hand
of the Majesty in heaven. Amen.**

26.27 CREED
From John 1†

Let us declare our faith in the Son of God:

**In the beginning was the Word,
and the Word was with God,
and the Word was God.
Through him all things were made;
without him nothing was made
that has been made.
In him was life,
and that life was the light of all people.**

**The Word became flesh
and lived for a while among us;
we have seen his glory,
the glory of the one and only Son
who came from the Father,
full of grace and truth. Amen.**

26.33 FOR THE HOMELESS
From 'New Every Morning'

Lord Jesus Christ, born in a stable:
hear the cry of the homeless and refugee,
and so move our wills
  by your Holy Spirit
that we may not rest content
until all have found home and livelihood;
for your name's sake. **Amen.**

26.34 FOR HEARTS AND HOMES
      OPEN TO CHRIST
Roger Pickering

Loving Father,
we thank you for the gift of your Son,
whose birth at Bethlehem
  we now prepare to celebrate:
make our hearts and our homes
  always open to him –
that he may dwell with us for ever,
and we may serve him gladly
all our days,
  to the honour and glory of your name.
Amen.

26.42 RESPONSIVE THANKSGIVING
From 'Worship Now'

For the birth of Jesus your Son, our
Saviour, cradled in the manger at
Bethlehem;
we thank you, heavenly Father.

For the love and gentle care of Mary, his
mother, most blessed of all women:
we thank you, heavenly Father.

For shepherds keeping watch over their
flocks by night, who came with haste to
worship Christ, the new-born King:
we thank you, heavenly Father.

For wise men from the East, who
followed the star and presented him with
their gifts of gold and frankincense and
myrrh:
we thank you, heavenly Father.

For the light and love of this Christmas
season, in our hearts and in our homes,
bringing joy and gladness to us all:
we thank you, heavenly Father.

And in our joyful gratitude we join our
voices with the angels who are always
singing to you:
Holy, holy, holy Lord
God of power and might,
heaven and earth are full of your glory;
hosanna in the highest. Amen.

26.43 THANKSGIVING
National Christian Education Council

God our Father, we listen again to the
story of Christmas, and we are glad that
Jesus has come to be our saviour and our
friend.

We hear how Mary laid her baby in a
manger. Jesus has come:
thank you, Father.

We hear how the angels sang over the
Bethlehem hills: 'Glory to God; peace for
the world.' Jesus has come:
thank you, Father.

We hear how the shepherds hurried to
see that what the angel said was true.
Jesus has come:
thank you, Father.

We hear how the wise men came to bring
their worship and their precious gifts.
Jesus has come:
thank you, Father.

O God,
we thank you
that Jesus has come to be our saviour
    and our friend:
we welcome him with love,
and worship him with gladness,
for your glory's sake. Amen.

26.44 THANKSGIVING
Liturgical Commission

We thank you, Father,
giver of all good things,
for the joy of this season of Christmas,
for the good news of a Saviour,
and for the wonder
  of the Word made flesh,
your Son, Jesus Christ, our Lord. **Amen.**

26.45   THANKSGIVING
AT COMMUNION
Liturgical Commission

We thank you, Father, God of love,
for the signs of your love on this table,
for your love made known
    through all the world
and shining on us
in the face of Jesus Christ, our Lord.
Amen.

26.48   ACCLAMATION
From Isaiah 25†

O Lord,
we exalt and praise your name,
for you are faithful to us
and have done marvellous things –
    things promised long ago.
For certain, you are our God:
we trust in you and you save us;
through Jesus our redeemer. **Amen.**

At a Baptism

27.1   GREETING
From Titus 1†

Grace and peace to you from God our
Father and Jesus Christ our Saviour.
Amen.

27.8   RESPONSE
From Ezekiel 47†

I saw water flowing from the right side of
the temple; the water flowed, it brought
God's life and his salvation. The people
sang in joyful praise:
Alleluia, alleluia!

27.9   RESPONSE
From 1 Corinthians 6†

Now you are washed, you are sanctified,
you are justified:
**in the name of the Lord Jesus Christ
and by the Spirit of our God. Amen.**

27.10   RESPONSE
From Romans 8†

There is now no condemnation for those
who are in Christ Jesus:
**the Spirit of life has set us free
from the law of sin and death. Amen.**

27.11   RESPONSE
From 1 Samuel 1 and Psalm 127†

Hannah said 'I prayed for this child, and
the Lord has granted me what I asked of
him':
**Children are a gift from the Lord;
they are his blessing. Amen.**

27.12   RESPONSE
From 1 Corinthians 6†

Now you are washed, you are sanctified,
you are justified:
**in the name of the Lord Jesus Christ
and by the Spirit of our God. Amen.**

27.14   PRAISE
From Psalm 34†

Glorify the Lord with me:
let us praise his name together.

27.15   PRAISE
From Psalm 107†

Give thanks to God, for he is good;
his love endures for ever.

Let those whom the Lord has redeemed
repeat these words of praise:
**O thank the Lord for his love
and the wonderful things he has done!
Amen.**

27.16 CONFESSION
From 1 John 1†

If we say that we have no sin, we deceive
ourselves, and the truth is not in us:
If we confess our sins,
God will keep his promise
and do what is right –
he will forgive us our sins
and cleanse us
    from every kind of wrong.
Father, have mercy on us
through Jesus Christ our Lord. Amen.

27.19 COLLECT
Baptism, ASB 1980

Almighty God,
we thank you for our fellowship
in the household of faith
with all those who have been baptized
    in your name.
Keep us faithful to our baptism,
and so make us ready for that day
when the whole creation
shall be made perfect in your Son
our Saviour, Jesus Christ. **Amen.**

27.20 PSALM
Psalm 113. 1–9†

The ministers/leaders may divide at A and B

A Praise the Lord:
    praise the Lord!

B You servants of the Lord, praise his
    name:
    let the name of the Lord be praised,
    both now and for evermore!

A From the rising of the sun to the
    place where it sets:
    the name of the Lord be praised!

B The Lord is exalted above the earth:
    his glory over the heavens.

A Who is like the Lord our God?
    He is throned in the heights above –

B Yet he bends down:
    yet he stoops to look at our world.

A He raises the poor from the dust:
    and lifts the needy from their sorrow.

B He honours the childless wife in her
    home:
    he makes her happy,
    the mother of children.

BOTH Praise the Lord:
    Amen.

27.22 CREED
From 1 Corinthians 12†

We believe in one Lord Jesus Christ,
one faith, one baptism,
one God and Father of us all,
who is in all and over all
and through all. Amen.

27.23 CREED
ASB 1980

Do you believe and trust in God the
Father, who made the world?
We believe and trust in him.

Do you believe and trust in his Son Jesus
Christ who redeemed mankind?
We believe and trust in him.

Do you believe and trust in his Holy
Spirit, who gives life to the people of
God?
We believe and trust in him.

This is the faith of the Church.
This is our faith.
We believe and trust in one God:
Father, Son, and Holy Spirit. Amen.

27.25 BLESSING
        OF THE CANDIDATE(S)
From Colossians 1†

The Lord God
fill you with the knowledge of his will;
his Spirit give you wisdom
    and understanding;
Christ strengthen you
    with his glorious power
so that you may be able to endure,
to be patient
and to give thanks to the Father
with joy in your heart(s). **Amen.**

**27.26   BLESSING
OF THE CANDIDATE(S)**
From 2 Timothy 1†

Hold firmly
to the true words you have been taught
as the example for you to follow,
and remain in the faith and love
   that are ours
in union with Christ Jesus,
through the power of the Holy Spirit
who lives in us. **Amen.**

**27.27   BLESSING
OF THE CANDIDATE(S)**
From 2 Timothy 2†

Be strong through the grace that is ours
in union with Christ Jesus;
take your part in suffering
as his loyal soldier(s);
and remember him
   who was raised from the dead,
Jesus Christ, our Lord and Saviour.
Amen.

27.29   INTERCESSION
From Isaiah 11†

We pray that *N* may bear fruit as a new
branch of the Vine which is Jesus Christ:

**May the spirit of the Lord
   rest upon him:
the spirit of wisdom and understanding,**

the spirit of counsel and power,
the spirit of knowledge
   and the fear of the Lord;
may he delight in the Lord. Amen.

27.30   THANKSGIVING
From 1 Peter 1†

We praise you,
O God and Father
   of our Lord Jesus Christ,
that in your great mercy
you have given us new birth
into a living hope
through the resurrection of Jesus Christ
from the dead,
and into an inheritance
that can never perish, spoil or fade –
kept in heaven for us,
who through faith
are shielded by God's power
until the coming of the salvation
that is ready to be revealed
   in the last time:
in this we greatly rejoice. **Amen.**

27.33   BLESSING
From 2 Peter 3†

May *you* grow in the grace and
knowledge of our Lord and Saviour Jesus
Christ:
**to him be glory
both now and for ever. Amen.**

At Holy Communion/The Lord's Supper

28.1   GREETING
From Romans 15†

Welcome one another as Christ has
welcomed you:
to God be the glory. Amen.

28.2   GREETING
From Ruth 2†

The Lord be with you:
the Lord bless you!

28.7   RESPONSE
From Matthew 5†

Blessed are the poor in spirit:
for theirs is the kingdom of heaven.

Blessed are those who hunger and thirst
for righteousness:
for they will be filled.

Praise the Lord:
The Lord's name be praised! Amen.

28.10 PRAISE
From Psalm 107†

Let us give thanks to the Lord for his
unfailing love
and the wonders he has done for us.

He satisfies the thirsty
and fills the hungry with good things.

28.11 COMMANDMENTS
From Mark 12†

Jesus said: Love the Lord your God with
all your heart and with all your soul and
with all your mind and with all your
strength; and love your neighbour as
yourself.
Lord,
we have broken your commandments:
forgive us, and help us to obey;
for your name's sake. Amen.

28.12 THE TEN COMMANDMENTS
From Exodus 20/Deuteronomy 5†

Let us hear the decrees and laws of the
Lord, learn them, and be sure to follow
them:
'You shall have no other gods but me':
Lord, help us to love you
with all our heart, all our soul,
all our mind and all our strength.

'You shall not make for yourself any
idol':
Lord, help us to worship you
in spirit and in truth.

'You shall not dishonour the name of the
Lord your God':
Lord, help us to honour you
with reverence and awe.

'Remember the Lord's day and keep it
holy':
Lord, help us to remember Christ
risen from the dead,
and to set our minds on things above,
not on things on the earth.

'Honour your father and your mother':
Lord, help us to live as your servants,
giving respect to all,

and love to our brothers and sisters
in Christ.

'You shall not murder'.
Lord, help us to be reconciled
with each other,
and to overcome evil with good.

'You shall not commit adultery':
Lord, help us to realise
that our body is a temple
of the Holy Spirit.

'You shall not steal':
Lord, help us to be honest in all we do,
and to care for those in need.

'You shall not be a false witness':
Lord, help us always to speak the truth.

'You shall not covet anything which
belongs to your neighbour':
Lord, help us to remember Jesus said,
'It is more blessed to give
than to receive',
and help us to love our neighbours
as ourselves;
for his sake. Amen.

28.13 ACT OF COMMITMENT (THE
TEN COMMANDMENTS)
From Exodus 20/Deuteronomy 5†

Let us resolve to follow the decrees and
the laws of the Lord:

Lord, we will have no other God
but you.

Lord, we will not make idols
for ourselves,
nor will we worship them.

Lord, we will not dishonour your name.

Lord, we will remember your day
and keep it holy.

Lord, we will honour our father
and our mother.

Lord, we will do no murder.

Lord, we will not commit adultery.

Lord, we will not steal.

Lord, we will not be a false witness.

Lord, we will not covet
anything that belongs to another.   →

May the awe of your presence and the
vision of your glory keep us from
sinning, for the sake of Jesus our
redeemer. **Amen.**

28.16 CONFESSION
BCP, adapted Editors

Almighty God,
Father of our Lord Jesus Christ,
maker and judge of all:
we confess the sins
which again and again
  we have so hurtfully committed
against you, our God and king.
By right you are angry
  and displeased at us.
We sincerely repent
and are truly sorry
for the wrong things we have done –
their memory is painful
and more than we can bear.
Have mercy on us, most merciful Father;
for Jesus' sake forgive us all that is past,
and renew our lives from this day
that we may serve you and please you,
and bring honour and glory
  to your name;
through Jesus Christ our Lord. Amen.

28.17 CONFESSION
From Psalm 51†

Lord God, have mercy on us,
according to your steadfast love;
and in your abundant mercy,
blot out our transgressions:
cleanse us from our sin,
create in us a clean heart and life,
and continually renew
a right spirit within us. Amen.

28.18 CONFESSION
From 1 John 1†

O God,
you have taught us
that if we say we have no sin
we deceive ourselves
and the truth is not in us:
we humbly confess our sins to you;

and we ask you to keep your promise
to forgive us our sins
and cleanse us
  from all unrighteousness;
through Jesus Christ our Lord. Amen.

28.20 WORDS OF COMFORT
*From Matthew 11, John 3, 1 Timothy 1, and
1 John 2†*

Jesus said, 'Come to me, all who are
heavy laden, and I will give you rest':
God so loved the world
that he gave his only Son,
that whoever believes in him
  should not perish
but have eternal life.

This saying is true and worthy of full
acceptance, that Christ Jesus came into
the world to save sinners.
If anyone sins
we have an advocate with the Father,
Jesus Christ the righteous;
and he is the propitiation for our sins.

28.22 COLLECT
Collect for Purity, adapted Editors

Almighty God,
you see into our hearts
and you know our minds;
we cannot hide our secrets from you:
cleanse our hearts and minds
  by the power of your Holy Spirit,
that we may perfectly love you
and worship you as you desire;
through Jesus Christ our Lord. **Amen.**

28.23 PSALM
Psalm 116.1–19†

The congregation may divide at A, B and C.

I love the Lord because he heard my
voice:
A **the Lord in mercy listened**
    to my prayers.

Because the Lord has turned his ear
to me:
B **I'll call on him**
    as long as I shall live.

The cords of death entangled me around:

c **the horrors of the grave
came over me.**

But then I called upon the Lord my God:

A **I said to him:
'O Lord, I beg you, save!'**

The Lord our God is merciful and good:

B **the Lord protects
the simple-hearted ones.**

The Lord saved me from death and stopped my tears:

c **he saved me from defeat
and picked me up.**

And so I walk before him all my days:

A **and live to love and praise
his holy name.**

What shall I give the Lord for all his grace?

B **I'll take his saving cup,
and pay my vows.**

Within the congregation of his saints:

c **I'll offer him my sacrifice of praise.**

Praise the Lord:

ALL **Amen, amen!**

28.26   CREED
ASB 1980, adapted

Let us affirm our faith in God:

**We believe and trust in God the Father
who made the world.**

**We believe and trust in his Son
Jesus Christ,
who redeemed mankind.**

**We believe and trust in his Holy Spirit,
who gives life to the people of God.**

**We believe and trust in one God:
Father, Son, and Holy Spirit. Amen.**

28.27   INTERCESSION
ASB 1980

Let us pray for the whole Church of God in Christ Jesus, and for all people according to their needs:

O God, our creator and preserver, we pray for people of every race, and in every kind of need: make your ways known on earth, your saving power among all nations. (Especially we pray for . . .) Lord, in your mercy
hear our prayer.

We pray for your Church throughout the world: guide and govern us by your Holy Spirit, that all who profess and call themselves Christians may be led into the way of truth, and hold the faith in unity of spirit, in the bond of peace, and in righteousness of life. (Especially we pray for . . .) Lord, in your mercy
hear our prayer.

We commend to your fatherly goodness all who are anxious or distressed in mind or body; comfort and relieve them in their need; give them patience in their sufferings, and bring good out of their troubles. (Especially we pray for . . .) Merciful Father,
**accept these prayers
for the sake of your Son,
our Saviour Jesus Christ. Amen.**

28.28   FOR VARIOUS PEOPLE
Editors

God our Father, grant us the help of your Spirit in our prayers for the salvation of humankind. We pray for the whole church, that in faith and unity it may constantly be renewed by your Holy Spirit for mission and service. Lord, in your mercy,
hear our prayer.

We pray for the peoples of the world and the leaders of the nations, that they may seek justice, freedom and peace for all. Lord, in your mercy,
hear our prayer.

→

We pray for our own country and for all who have authority and influence, that they may serve in wisdom, honesty and compassion. Lord, in your mercy,
hear our prayer.

We pray for the communities in which we live and work, that there we may use your gifts to set people free from drudgery and poverty, and together find joy in your creation. Lord, in your mercy,
hear our prayer.

We pray for those who are ill . . . , for those in sorrow . . . , for the anxious, the lonely, the despairing, the persecuted, and for all who suffer from cruelty, injustice or neglect, that they may find strength and hope. Lord, in your mercy,
hear our prayer.

We pray for the life and witness of this church and all its members, that we may serve you in holiness throughout our lives.
Lord hear our prayers,
in the strong name
   of Jesus Christ. Amen.

28.30   PEACE
From Romans 1†

Grace and peace to you from God our Father and from the Lord Jesus Christ:
peace be with you. Amen.

28.31   PEACE
From Romans 15†

The God of peace be with you all. **Amen.**

28.32   PEACE
From 1 Corinthians 1†

*Here the local community may be named

To the church of God *in . . . *, to* those sanctified in Christ Jesus and called to be holy, to all those everywhere who call on the name of our Lord Jesus Christ – their Lord and ours: grace and peace to you from God our Father and the Lord Jesus Christ. **Amen.**

28.33   PEACE
From 2 Corinthians 13†

Be of one mind, live in peace; the God of love and peace be with you. **Amen.**

28.34   PEACE
From Galatians 1†

Grace and peace be with you from God our Father and the Lord Jesus Christ, who gave himself for our sins according to the will of our God and Father; to whom be glory for ever and ever. **Amen.**

28.35   PEACE
From Galatians 6†

Peace and mercy to the people of God.
Amen.

28.36   PEACE
From Ephesians 6†

Peace to our sisters and brothers, and love with faith from God the Father and the Lord Jesus Christ. **Amen.**

28.37   PEACE
From Ephesians 6†

Grace to all who love our Lord Jesus Christ with an undying love. **Amen.**

28.38   PEACE
From Philippians 4 and Philemon†

The grace of the Lord Jesus Christ be with your spirit. **Amen.**

28.39   PEACE
From 2 Timothy 1†

Grace, mercy and peace from God the Father and Christ Jesus our Lord. **Amen.**

28.40   PEACE
From 2 Timothy 4†

The Lord be with your spirit:
grace be with you. Amen.

28.41 PEACE
From 1 Thessalonians†

Grace and peace to you from God our Father and the Lord Jesus Christ. **Amen.**

28.42 PEACE
From Titus 1†

Grace and peace from God our Father and Christ Jesus our Saviour. **Amen.**

28.43 PEACE
From Philemon 1†

Grace to you and peace from God our Father and the Lord Jesus Christ. **Amen.**

28.44 PEACE
From 1 Peter 1†

Grace and peace be yours in abundance: **praise be to God!**

28.45 PEACE
From 2 Peter 1†

Grace and peace be yours in abundance through the knowledge of God and of Jesus our Lord. **Amen.**

28.46 PEACE
From 2 John†

Grace, mercy and peace from God the Father and from Jesus Christ, the Father's Son, be with you in truth and love. **Amen.**

28.47 PEACE
From Jude†

You are loved by God the Father and kept by Jesus Christ: mercy, peace and love be yours for ever. **Amen.**

28.48 PEACE (EASTER)
From Revelation 1†

Grace and peace to you from him who is, and who was, and who is to come, [and from the seven spirits before his throne,] and from Jesus Christ, who is the faithful witness, the firstborn from the dead: **Alleluia! Amen.**

28.49 PEACE (EASTER)
From Revelation 1†

Grace and peace to you from Jesus Christ, who is the faithful witness, the firstborn from the dead. **Amen.**

28.50 PEACE
From Revelation 1†

Grace and peace to you from him who is, and who was, and who is to come. **Amen.**

28.51 PEACE
From Revelation 22†

The grace of the Lord Jesus be with God's people. **Amen.**

28.52 PEACE/GREETING
From 1 Peter 5†

Peace to all of you in Christ: greet one another with [a kiss of] love. **Amen.**

28.53 PEACE/GREETING
From 3 John†

Peace to you all . . . greet your friends by name.

28.54 GREETING
From Romans 15†

Welcome one another as Christ has welcomed you: **to God be the glory. Amen.**

28.55 ASCRIPTION
From 1 Chronicles 29†

Yours, Lord, is the greatness, the power,
the glory, the splendour and the majesty:
**everything in heaven and on earth is
yours.**

Everything comes from you,
and of your own do we give you.

28.57 INVITATION
Editors

Come to this table, not because you are
strong, but because you are weak; come,
not because any goodness of your own
gives you a right to come, but because
you need mercy and help; come, because
you love the Lord a little and would like
to love him more; come, not because you
are worthy to approach him, but because
he died for sinners; come, because he
loved you and gave himself for you:
**Your death, O Lord, we commemorate,
your resurrection we proclaim,
your coming again in glory
    we anticipate:
glory to you,
living saviour and Lord! Amen.**

28.58 PRAYER OF APPROACH
Editors

**Jesus,
we come to this your table
not because we are strong,
but because we are weak;
not because any goodness of our own
gives us the right to come,
but because we need your mercy
    and your help;
not because of anything
    we have achieved,
but because you died for sinners.
Glory be to you,
    our living saviour and Lord. Amen.**

28.61 DIALOGUE
From Ruth 2 and Psalm 107†

The Lord be with you:
the Lord bless you.

Let us give thanks to the Lord for his
unfailing love
and the wonders he has done for us.

He satisfies the thirsty
**and fills the hungry with good things.
Amen.**

28.62 DIALOGUE
ICET

The Lord is here:
his Spirit is with us.

Lift up your hearts:
we lift them to the Lord.

Let us give thanks to the Lord our God:
it is right to give him thanks and praise.

28.63 DOXOLOGY
From Revelation 4 and 5†

Let us give glory to God:

Our Lord and God, you are worthy to
receive glory, honour, and power; for
you created all things, and by your will
they were given existence and life:
Glory to God in the highest!

O Lamb of God, you are worthy to
receive wisdom, strength, and praise, for
by your death you bought for God
people from every tribe, language, nation
and race:
Glory to God in the highest!

You have made them a kingdom of
priests to serve our God, and they shall
rule on earth:
Glory to God in the highest!

To him who sits upon the throne
and to the Lamb,
be praise and honour,
glory and power,
for ever and ever! Amen.

28.65 THANKSGIVING (END OF YEAR)
Editors

For the year that is past:
Lord, we thank you.

For your mercies every day:
Lord, we thank you.

For new discoveries of your grace, and fresh opportunities to do your work:
Lord, we thank you.

For your strength to survive hurt and sorrow, and that you pick us up when we fall:
Lord, we thank you.

For our life in Christ which gives us hope for the future:
Lord, we thank you.

**Lord,
we thank you that you walk beside us –
your mighty hand to uphold us,
your heart of love to guide us,
your outstretched arms
   to bring us to our journey's end.**

28.66 THANKSGIVING (END/BEGINNING OF YEAR)
Lancelot Andrewes (1555–1626) adapted

Blessing and honour,
thanksgiving and praise,
more than we can utter,
more than we can conceive,
be to your glorious name, O God,
Father, Son and Holy Spirit,
by all angels, all people, all creation,
for ever.

28.67 THANKSGIVING (EPIPHANY ETC.)
From Psalm 117†

O Lord of all the nations,
we your people praise you and extol you;
for your love towards us is great
and your faithfulness endures for ever.

28.70 THANKSGIVING (LIFE OF PRAYER/FORGIVENESS)
From Psalm 118†

God our Father, we thank you,
for you are good,
and your love endures for ever;
we thank you
   that you have heard our cry to you
and set us free;
we thank you that you are with us,
and we need not be afraid;
we thank you that you have answered us
and become our salvation.

28.71 THANKSGIVING (THE FAMILY ETC.)
From Psalm 145†

God our Father,
gracious and compassionate,
slow to anger and rich in mercy:
we thank you
   that you keep your promises,
and love all that you have made;
you uphold those who fall,
and lift up those who are bowed low;
you open your hand
and satisfy the desires of your people
who fear you,
you hear our cry and save us.

28.73 THANKSGIVING (EASTER)
From 1 Peter 1†

Praise be to you, O God our Father:
for in your great mercy
you have given us new birth
   into a living hope
through the resurrection from the dead
of Jesus Christ our Lord.

28.75   THANKSGIVING
(GOD'S CREATION)
Editors

Gracious Father and creator, the variety of beauty and colour in the world often leaves us speechless; the rolling hills, the mighty seas, the desert plains and the succulent green pastures, all proclaim your power and creative provision. O Lord our God:
we praise and adore you.

We praise you for the warming sun, the growth-making rain, the freshness of a new morning and the calm of a still evening: all proclaim your purpose and your pleasure. O Lord our God:
we praise and adore you.

We praise you for your Son, our Saviour, Jesus Christ: through him we have received pardon for our sin and the joy of salvation; for he lived and died and rose again to redeem us. O Lord our God:
we praise and adore you.

**For all the work of your hands,
and for every gift
   from your heart of love,
we exalt your holy name.**

28.76   THANKSGIVING
(JESUS IS LORD)
From Revelation 4†

You are worthy, O Lord our God:
to receive glory and honour and power.

For you created all things:
**and by your will they existed
and were created.**

You are worthy, O Christ, for you were slain:
**and by your blood
you ransomed us for God.**

From every tribe and tongue and people and nation:
**you made us a kingdom of priests
to serve our God.**

To him who sits upon the throne, and to the Lamb:

be blessing and honour
and glory and might.

28.79   THANKSGIVING
(SEA THEME/HOLIDAYS)
From Psalm 136†

O God our Father, we thank you, for you are good:
Lord, your love endures for ever.

We thank you that you are the God of gods; we thank you that you are the Lord of lords:
Lord, your love endures for ever.

We thank you that you do great wonders; that by your understanding you made the skies and spread out the earth and sea:
Lord, your love endures for ever.

We thank you that you made the lights of heaven – the sun to rule the day, and the moon and stars to govern the night:
Lord, your love endures for ever.

We thank you that you have remembered us in our humiliation; that through your Son Jesus Christ you have freed us from our enemies, the power of evil and of death:
Lord, your love endures for ever.

28.80   THANKSGIVING (GOD'S LOVE
TO US/HOLY COMMUNION)
From Psalm 36†

We thank you, our Father,
that your love reaches to the heavens,
and your faithfulness to the skies;
that your justice is like the great deep.
Without price are your unfailing mercies;
we feast on your goodness
and drink from the river of your blessing.

28.81   THANKSGIVING
(INVITATION TO FAITH)
From Psalm 118†

O God our Father, we thank you,
for you are good,
and your love endures for ever:
we thank you

that you have heard our cry to you
and set us free;
we thank you that you are with us,
and we need not be afraid;
we thank you that you have answered us
and become our salvation in Jesus.

28.82 THANKSGIVING
(THE CARING CHURCH)
Psalm 138.1†

We thank you, God our Father,
   with all our hearts
and sing to you our songs and hymns;
we bow before you in worship
   and praise you
because you have loved us
and shown yourself faithful;
your word is as mighty as your name –
and when we call to you,
you answer our prayer
and give us the strength we need.
Though you are very high,
yet you care for the lowly,
and the proud cannot hide from you;
when we are surrounded by troubles
you keep us safe.

28.83 THANKSGIVING(MISSIONARY/
WORLDWIDE CHURCH)
From Revelation 5†

We thank you, our Father,
that you sent your Son, Jesus Christ
to die for us
and by his blood to ransom us
from every tribe and tongue
and people and nation;
and to make us
a kingdom of priests
to serve our God.

28.84 THANKSGIVING (RENEWAL)
From 1 Corinthians 12†

We thank you, O God for our unity in
diversity:

For different kinds of gifts:
but the same Spirit.

For different kinds of service:
but the same Lord.

For different kinds of working:
but the same God.

**Thank you, God our Father,
that you work in us
in all these ways.**

28.86 THANKSGIVING
(CHURCH ANNIVERSARY)
From Revelation 15†

Glory be to you, O God,
Father, Son, and Holy Spirit –
you have power, wisdom and majesty:
receive from us
honour, glory, worship and blessing.
Great and marvellous are your works,
just and true are your ways:
blessing and honour and
   glory and power
be to him who reigns upon the throne,
and to the Lamb,
through the one eternal Spirit,
now and for ever.

28.87 THANKSGIVING
('LAMMAS'/HARVEST)
D. L. Couper, adapted

Let us give thanks to the Lord our God:
It is right to give him thanks and praise.

It is indeed right,
it is our duty and our joy,
at all times and in all places
to give you thanks and praise,
holy Father, heavenly King,
almighty and eternal God,
creator of heaven and earth,
through Jesus Christ our Lord:
for you have provided for us
and prospered us
and called us to be your fellow-workers.
You have ripened our first-fruits
with the spring rain
and the warmth of the summer sun;
you have given us
all things richly to enjoy
and have blessed the work of our hands.

28.89 THANKSGIVING (CHRISTIAN
           CONFLICT AND CHARACTER)
From Psalm 138

God our Father,
we thank you with all our heart
and bow before you in worship,
because you have loved us
and shown yourself faithful;
your word is as mighty as your name,
and when we call to you
you answer our prayer
and give us the strength we need;
though you are very high,
yet you care for the lowly,
and the proud cannot hide from you;
when we are surrounded by troubles
you keep us safe:
Father, we thank you
that your love is eternal,
and you will complete in us
the work you have begun.

28.90 THANKSGIVING
           (HEAVEN/GOD'S PEOPLE)
From 1 Peter 1†

We thank you, O God our Father:
that in your great mercy
you have given us new birth
into a living hope
through the resurrection from the dead
of Jesus Christ our Lord.

28.92 THANKSGIVING
           (WORD OF GOD)
From Romans 11†

O Lord God our Father,
we thank you
for the riches of your wisdom
   and your knowledge.
How unsearchable are your judgements;
your paths beyond tracing out!
Who has known your mind
or been your counsellor?
Who has ever given anything to you
that you should repay?
For from you and through you
and to you are all things.
To you be the glory for ever!

28.93 THANKSGIVING (CHRISTMAS)
'Worship Now' and Liturgical Commission

For the birth of Jesus your Son, our
Saviour, cradled in the manger at
Bethlehem;
we thank you, heavenly Father.

For the love and gentle care of Mary, his
mother, most blessed of all women:
we thank you, heavenly Father.

For shepherds keeping watch over their
flocks by night, who came with haste to
worship Christ, the new-born King:
we thank you, heavenly Father.

For wise men from the East, who
followed the star and presented him with
their gifts of gold and frankincense and
myrrh:
we thank you, heavenly Father.

For the light and love of this Christmas
season, in our hearts and in our homes,
bringing joy and gladness to us all:
we thank you, heavenly Father.

And in our joyful gratitude we join our
voices with the angels who are always
singing to you:
**Holy, holy, holy Lord
God of power and might,
heaven and earth are full of your glory;
hosanna in the highest. Amen.**

And now we thank you,
   Father, God of love,
for the signs of your love on this table,
for your love made known
   through all the world
and shining on us
in the face of Jesus Christ.

28.95 THANKSGIVING
           (LOCAL FESTIVALS)
From 1 Chronicles 29†

Lord God of our fathers,
may you be praised for ever and ever!

You are great and powerful, glorious,
splendid and majestic: Lord God of our
fathers,
may you be praised for ever and ever!

Everything in heaven and earth is yours,
and you are king, supreme ruler over all:
Lord God of our fathers,
may you be praised for ever and ever!

All riches and wealth come from you;
you rule everything by your strength and
power: Lord God of our fathers,
may you be praised for ever and ever!

Now, our God,
we give you thanks,
and praise your glorious name.

28.96 WORDS OF INSTITUTION
From 1 Corinthians 11†

Our Lord Jesus Christ,
in the same night that he was betrayed,
took bread,
and when he had given thanks
he broke it and said,
'This is my body, which is for you;
do this to remember me'.

In the same way, after supper
he took the cup, saying,
'This cup
   is the new covenant in my blood;
do this, whenever you drink it,
to remember me'. **Amen.**

And there may be added:

Whenever you eat this bread and drink
this cup, you proclaim the Lord's death
until he comes. **Amen.**

28.97 WORDS OF INSTITUTION
Song: Janet Lunt © Mustard Seed Music

And now we thank you for the symbols
of Christ's body broken and blood shed:

   Broken for me, broken for you,
   the body of Jesus broken for you.

He offered his body,
he poured out his soul,
Jesus was broken
that we might be whole:
   Broken for me . . .

Come to my table
and with me dine,
eat of my bread
and drink of my wine:
   Broken for me . . .

This is my body
given for you,
eat it remembering
I died for you:
   Broken for me . . .

This is my blood
I shed for you,
for your forgiveness,
making you new:
   Broken for me . . .

28.98 COMMUNION PRAYER
Editors et al

God our Father, we give you our thanks
(at this time especially for . . .) and we
rejoice to praise you through Jesus Christ
our Lord.
Through him you made us,
through him you set us free
   from sin and death,
through him you gave us
   your Holy Spirit,
and called us into one family.

So, Father, by the same Spirit, let us who
take this bread and wine, receive the
body and blood of Christ.

For when the time came for him to be
lifted up to die and so to enter his glory,
he gathered his disciples and took bread
and gave thanks to you; then he broke it
and gave it to them saying, 'Take, eat:
this is my body which is given for you;
do this to remember me'. After supper he
took the cup and gave thanks. He gave it
to them saying, 'Drink this, all of you:
this is my blood of the new covenant,
shed for you and for many that sins may
be forgiven; do this every time you drink
it, to remember me'.

Now as we look for his coming, we
celebrate with this bread and wine, his
one perfect sacrifice, proclaiming his
death for our salvation and rejoicing in

the power of his resurrection, until we share the fellowship of his Kingdom.
Father,
accept the thanks and praise
of your children
in this sacred feast;
renew us by your Holy Spirit,
and make us one
in Christ Jesus our Lord. Amen.

28.99   RESPONSE (SANCTUS)

With the whole family in heaven and on earth we praise and adore you, saying:
Holy, holy, holy Lord,
God of power and might,
heaven and earth are full of your glory.
Hosanna in the highest. Amen.

28.100   RESPONSE (SANCTUS)
From Revelation 5

Holy, holy, holy is the Lord,
holy is the Lord God almighty,
who was and is and is to come;
holy, holy, holy is the Lord.

28.101   RESPONSE (SANCTUS)
From Revelation 5

Holy, holy, holy
is the Lord God almighty,
who was, and is
and is to come. **Amen.**

28.102   RESPONSE (SANCTUS)
From Isaiah 6†

Holy, holy, holy
is the Lord God almighty:
the whole earth is full of his glory.
Amen.

28.103   RESPONSE
From Revelation 5†

Worthy is the Lamb, who was slain, to receive power and wealth and wisdom and strength and honour and glory and praise:
to him who sits upon the throne
and to the Lamb

be praise and honour
and glory and power
for ever and ever. Amen.

28.104   RESPONSE
            (ESPECIALLY EASTER)
From 2 Corinthians 13†

In weakness Christ was put to death on the Cross:
by God's power he lives!

28.105   FOR CHRIST'S PRESENCE
Robert Runcie

Come, Lord,
in the fullness of your risen presence,
and make yourself known
    to your people again
through the breaking of the bread,
and the sharing of the cup. **Amen.**

28.106   FOR CHRIST'S PRESENCE
F. W. Street

Come to us, Lord Jesus,
in your risen power,
when we receive the bread of life
    and the cup of salvation;
cleanse our hearts from sin,
that they may be worthy
    of so great a guest;
and keep us firm in your love,
for your great name's sake. **Amen.**

28.107   FOR THE HOLY SPIRIT
Editors

Come, Holy Spirit:
speak to us of Jesus,
heal us and renew us,
strengthen our wills to obey,
warm our hearts
with love for one another;
bring glory to the name
    of our mighty God. **Amen.**

28.108   THE LORD'S PRAYER
ICET, adapted ASB 1980

**Our Father in heaven,
hallowed be your name,
your kingdom come,
your will be done,
on earth as in heaven.
Give us today our daily bread.
Forgive us our sins
as we forgive those
   who sin against us.
Lead us not into temptation
but deliver us from evil.**

**For the kingdom, the power,
   and the glory are yours
now and for ever. Amen.**

28.109   SENTENCE (ESPECIALLY
              LENT AND PASSIONTIDE)
1 Corinthians 11.26†

*At the breaking of the bread and the taking of
the wine:*

Whenever you eat this bread and drink
this cup, you proclaim the Lord's death
until he comes. **Amen.**

28.110   RESPONSES
From John 6 and 15†

At the breaking of the bread

Jesus said, 'I am the bread of life: those
who come to me will never grow hungry,
and those who believe in me will never
be thirsty.'
**'Lord, give us this bread for ever.'
Amen.**

At the sharing of the wine

Jesus said, 'I am the true vine . . . remain
in me, and I will remain in you.' **Amen.**

28.111   RESPONSES
From Luke 22 and Mark 14†

At the breaking of the bread

Jesus said, 'I have eagerly desired to eat
this passover with you before I suffer; for
I tell you, I will not eat it again until it
finds fulfilment in the kingdom of God.'

'Do this in memory of me.' **Amen.**

At the sharing of the wine

Jesus said, 'I tell you the truth, I will not
drink again of the fruit of the vine until
that day when I drink it anew in the
kingdom of God.'

'Take this and share it among you.'
Amen.

28.112   RESPONSES
From 1 Corinthians 10†

At the breaking of the bread

The bread that we break:
**is a sharing in the body of Christ.
Amen.**

At the sharing of the wine

The cup of thanksgiving for which we
give thanks:
**is a sharing in the blood of Christ.
Amen.**

28.113   RESPONSES
From John 6†

At the breaking of the bread

Jesus said, 'The bread of God is he who
comes down from heaven and gives life
to the world':
**Lord, from now on give us this bread.
Amen.**

At the sharing of the wine

Jesus said, 'Whoever believes in me will
never be thirsty'.
**Lord, we have seen and we believe.
Amen.**

28.114   RESPONSES
From John 6†

At the breaking of the bread

Jesus said, 'Just as the living Father sent
me and I live because of the Father, so
the one who feeds on me will live
because of me':
**This is the bread
that came down from heaven. Amen.**

$\rightarrow$

At the sharing of the wine

Jesus said, 'Unless you can eat the flesh of the Son of Man and drink his blood, you have no life in you'.
This is the blood of eternal life. Amen.

28.115   RESPONSES
From 1 Corinthians 10†

At the breaking of the bread

We break the bread and eat
to share in the body of Christ

So we who eat are one:
for we all share one bread.

At the sharing of the wine

We give thanks for the cup, and drink
to share in the blood of Christ. Amen.

28.116   RESPONSES
From 1 Corinthians 11. 24,25†

At the breaking of the bread

When he had given thanks, Jesus said 'This is my body which is for you: do this in remembrance of me.' **Amen.**

At the taking of the cup

In the same way he took the cup and said, 'This cup is the new covenant in my blood: drink this always in remembrance of me.' **Amen.**

28.117   INVITATION
From Hebrews 10†

Draw near with a sincere heart and a sure faith, purged from your guilt and washed clean through the blood of Christ; hold on to your hope and trust the promises of God. **Amen.**

28.118   WORDS OF
              ADMINISTRATION
Editors

At the giving of the bread

Receive this bread as the token that Jesus loves you, and died for you. **Amen.**

At the giving of the wine

Let this wine cleanse you by the blood of Christ, and fill you with his love. **Amen.**

28.120   THANKSGIVING AFTER
              COMMUNION
Liturgical Commission

Eternal Father,
we thank you for refreshing us
with these heavenly gifts:
may our communion
strengthen us in faith,
build us up in hope,
and make us grow in love;
for the sake of Jesus Christ our Lord.
Amen.

28.122   DOXOLOGY
From Romans 16†

Glory to God
who alone is all–wise;
through Jesus Christ, for ever! **Amen.**

28.126   DISMISSAL
From 'A New Zealand Prayer Book'

Let us bless the Lord:
thanks be to God.

The almighty and merciful God bless us and keep us now and for ever. **Amen.**

28.127   DISMISSAL
From 1 Corinthians 16†

Let all who love the Lord be blessed:
come, O Lord.

Love to you all in Christ Jesus:
the grace of the Lord Jesus be with you. Amen.

At Local Festivals, For the Peace of the World

29.1 GREETING
From Romans 1

Grace and peace to you from God our Father and from the Lord Jesus Christ. **Amen.**

29.7 RESPONSE†
From Galatians 1 †

Grace and peace to you from God our Father and the Lord Jesus Christ:
to whom be glory for ever and ever. Amen.

29.8 RESPONSE
From Amos 5†

Let justice roll on like a river:
**and righteousness
like a never failing stream. Amen.**

29.9 RESPONSE
From 2 Chronicles †

Lord, God of our fathers, you are the God of heaven; you rule over all the kingdoms of the nations:
**power and might are in your hand,
and no-one can withstand you.**

We have no power to face the perils that confront us:
**we do not know what to do,
but our eyes are upon you, O Lord.
Amen.**

29.10 RESPONSE
From Revelation 1†

Grace and peace to you from Jesus Christ, the ruler of the kings of the earth. **Amen.**

29.11 APPROACH (CIVIC OCCASION)
From Psalm 138†

Lord, we worship you with all our heart; before the powers of the universe we sing your praises.

We come into your house and honour your name because of your love and faithfulness; for you have exalted your name and your word above all things. We worship you with all our heart;
your love endures for ever.

When we called to you, you answered us; you gave us courage. We worship you with all our heart;
your love endures for ever.

O may the leaders of the nations praise you, Lord, when they hear the words of your mouth – let them too sing of your ways, for your glory is very great. Though you are so high yet you look upon the lowly – while you distance yourself from the proud. We worship you with all our heart;
your love endures for ever. Amen.

29.14 PRAISE
From Psalm 134†

All you servants of the Lord:
praise the Lord.

You who come into his house to worship him:
praise the Lord.

Lift up your hands in his presence:
praise the Lord.

May the Lord, the maker of heaven and earth, bless you in this holy place. **Amen.**

29.15 PRAISE
From Psalm 67†

Let the people praise you, O God;
let all the people praise you!

Let your ways be known on earth;
your saving power in all the world!

29.16 CONFESSION
From Jeremiah 14

**O Lord,
we acknowledge our own wickedness
and the guilt of our society;
we have sinned against you.
For the sake of your name
do not despise us;
remember your new covenant
    in Jesus our redeemer
and forgive us our sin;
for his name's sake. Amen.**

29.17 CONFESSION
Editors

We confess our sins and selfishness, our pride, our greed, the evil divisions we create and sustain. O Lord of mercy, we put our hope in you:
**forgive us and help us
for your name's sake.**

We confess our share in the world's wrong, and our failure to strive for that universal peace and justice which is your will. O Lord of mercy, we put our hope in you:
**forgive us and help us
for your name's sake.**

We confess we have not loved you with our whole heart nor our neighbours as ourselves. O Lord of mercy, we put our hope in you:
**forgive us and help us
for your name's sake.**

**Release us from our sins
by the cross of Christ
and strengthen us for his service
by the power of your Spirit. Amen.**

29.18 CONFESSION
Editor

Lord God, our maker and our redeemer, this is your world and we are your people: come among us and save us.

Where we have wilfully misused your gifts of creation, be merciful, Lord:
forgive us and help us.

Where we have seen the ill-treatment of others and have not gone to their aid, be merciful, Lord:
forgive us and help us.

Where we have condoned the lie in our society, and failed to achieve justice or compassion, be merciful, Lord:
forgive us and help us.

Where we have heard for ourselves the good news of Christ, but have not shared it with our generation nor taught it to our children, be merciful, Lord:
forgive us and help us.

Where we have not loved you with all our heart, nor our neighbours as ourselves, be merciful, Lord:
forgive us and help us.

**O God,
forgive us for our lack of love,
and in your mercy make us
what you would have us be,
through Jesus Christ our Lord. Amen.**

29.21 PSALM
Psalm 122. 1–8

The congregation may divide at A – male voices, and B – female voices

I was glad when they said to me:
let us go to the house of the Lord!

Pray for the peace of Jerusalem:
A **may those who love our land be blessed.**

May there be peace in your homes:
B **and safety for our families.**

For the sake of those we love we say:
ALL **Let there be peace! Amen.**

29.22 PSALM
Psalm 124. 1–8

The congregation may divide at A, B and C

If the Lord had not been on our side
– now let Israel say:
If the Lord had not been on our side
A **when enemies attacked us,**
B **when their anger flared against us,**

c **they would have swallowed us
    alive.**
A **The flood would have engulfed us,**
B **the torrent
    would have swept over us,**
c **the waters would have drowned us.**

Praise the Lord:
A **who has not given us up
    to their teeth.**
B **We have escaped
    like a bird from the snare:**
c **the snare is broken and we are free.**

Our help is in the name of the Lord:
ALL **who made heaven and earth. Amen.**

29.25 CREED
ASB 1980

Do you believe in God the Father?
**We believe and trust in God the Father,
who made the world.**

Do you believe in God the Son?
**We believe and trust
in his Son Jesus Christ
who redeemed mankind.**

Do you believe in the Holy Spirit?
**We believe and trust in the Holy Spirit,
who gives life to the people of God.**

**We believe and trust in one God:
Father, Son, and Holy Spirit. Amen.**

29.26 ACT OF REMEMBRANCE
The congregation stands:

Let us remember in the presence of God
those who have died amid the tragedy of
war – those whom we knew and whose
memory we treasure, those mourned by
other loved ones. Let us celebrate all who
have lived and died in the service of their
fellow men and women.

They shall grow not old,
as we who are left grow old.

Age shall not weary them,
nor the years condemn.

At the going down of the sun,
and in the morning,
we will remember them:
we will remember them.
Silence is kept

29.27 FOR THOSE WHO SUFFER
         (REMEMBRANCE)
Editors

We pray for all who suffer as a result of
war:

For the injured and the disabled, for the
mentally distressed and for those whose
faith in God and in other people has been
weakened or destroyed, we lift our hearts
to you:
O Lord of mercy, hear our prayer.

For the homeless and refugees, for those
who are hungry, and for all who have
lost their livelihood and security, we lift
our hearts to you:
O Lord of mercy, hear our prayer.

For those who mourn their dead; for
those who have lost husband, wife,
children or parents, and especially for
those who have no hope in Christ to
sustain them in their grief, we lift our
hearts to you:
O Lord of mercy, hear our prayer.
Here follows a short silence, then:

O Lord, hear our prayer:
**for the sake of our Saviour, Jesus Christ.
Amen.**

29.29 REMEMBRANCE
Alan Gaunt

As we remember those who died in war
for the cause of peace:
Lord, make us peace-makers.

As we look to the future of our children
and grandchildren:
Lord, make us peace-makers.

As we think of the war torn, blood-
stained, sorrowful world:
Lord, make us peace-makers.

→

Lord, hear our prayer
and come to us in perfect love,
to drive away our fear;
in the name of the Prince of peace,
Jesus Christ our Lord. Amen.

29.30   INTERCESSION
Alan Gaunt, adapted Gill Tovar

Eternal God, we all need to know the power and the freedom of your healing. We pray for others in the knowledge of your love and forgiveness:

For all who are weighed down by a guilty conscience, for those who lack imagination, and for those who immerse themselves in activities so that they need never stand still to see themselves as they really are, Lord, in your mercy:
hear our prayer.

For those who have been stunned and shocked by death; for widows and orphaned children, especially for those who do not see how they can put their lives together again; and for those who suffer remorse because of what they did or failed to do, Lord, in your mercy:
hear our prayer.

For those whose bodies are being eaten away by disease – or fighting the invasion of infection; for those who suffer constant pain and continual discomfort, Lord, in your mercy:
hear our prayer.

For those who suffer the effects of war, political oppression or persecution; and for those who are unemployed, hungry, or dying through the failure of economic systems, Lord, in your mercy:
hear our prayer.

As we pray, we ask that we may take the joy and hope of being loved and forgiven and made whole into the world in the name of Christ – who loved life, and loved you, and loved all humankind and proved your love by his own self-sacrifice.

Make us like Christ,
so that through our lives
your love and forgiveness
  may be lived and proclaimed;
and your name honoured. Amen.

29.31   FOR FORGIVENESS
Alan Gaunt

For the wounds still inflicted on your children, Lord, forgive us and help us.

For infants who cry for food and get none; for the making of orphans and widows, Lord, forgive us:
forgive us and help us.

For those who mourn and are not comforted, for those who are guilty and are not convicted of sin, Lord, forgive us:
forgive us and help us.

For those who are lost and have no good news proclaimed to them, but are left to think you have rejected them, Lord, forgive us:
forgive us and help us.

Through the cross of Jesus
reconcile us to yourself
and to each other;
so that war may cease,
nation may speak peace to nation,
your will be done on earth
and your name honoured everywhere
  for ever. Amen.

29.32   FOR VICTIMS
Editors

Lord God, Father of mercy,
we pray for the innocent victims of war
and those held hostage in any place:
help us to remember them day by day.
May the light of Christ give them hope,
may the love of Christ
  give them strength,
and may the presence of your Holy Spirit
comfort and sustain them at all times.
Amen.

29.41 FOR GOOD GOVERNMENT
From 'A New Zealand Prayer Book'

Spirit of justice, creator Spirit:
help us to make and keep this country
a home for all its different peoples,
and grant to our government
    and all its representatives
imagination, skill and energy
that peace may grow among us,
through Jesus our Lord. **Amen.**

29.42 FOR QUEEN AND
        COMMONWEALTH
Editors

For the blessing of community in our
Nation and Commonwealth, and for
those who have used your gifts to
strengthen and enrich its life, with
grateful hearts:
we thank you, Lord.

For our sovereign lady, Queen Elizabeth,
for her long and tireless service to our
world-wide family of nations, for her
profession of faith in you by word and
deed, for her example of unselfish
devotion to duty, for her care for our
people, and for her concern for them at
all times and in all places, with grateful
hearts:
we thank you, Lord.

Continue in her and her family, we pray,
your royal gifts of service, the vision of
your will for her people, and wisdom to
fulfil her vocation of leadership in a
Commonwealth of many races. Give her
strength and courage to carry out the
duties of her calling.

**Grant her always the
assurance of your presence,
your power, and your love,
through Jesus Christ our Lord. Amen.**

29.43 FOR OUR NATIONAL LEADERS
Editors

Almighty God,
we pray for our Queen
and all leaders of our country,
that they may govern us wisely and well;
we pray for one another,
that we may live and work together
in love, mutual understanding and peace,
through Jesus Christ our Lord. **Amen.**

29.46 FOR OUR
        VILLAGE / TOWN / CITY
St Michael-le-Belfrey, York

Here the local community is named

Heavenly Father,
we thank you for . . . *
and for every person who lives here.
Help us to care more for our community,
to share your love,
and to stand for your truth:
through Jesus Christ our Lord. **Amen.**

29.50 FOR THOSE WHO SERVE
        OUR COMMUNITY
Editors

Almighty God, you have taught us to
intercede for others:

For those who guard the health of our
people and tend the sick at home and in
hospital, for scientists who seek ways of
combating disease, and for all engaged in
administration, Lord, hear our prayer:
Lord, bless them and help them.

For those who bear witness to Jesus in
their work of healing, Lord, hear our
prayer:
Lord, bless them and help them.

For police and customs, for ambulance
and fire officers, for the military and
those in our land who keep us in safety,
Lord, hear our prayer:
Lord, bless them and help them.

For those responsible for the
maintenance of law and order –
legislators, lawyers, judges, probation
officers, prison staff and the police, Lord,
hear our prayer:
Lord, bless them and help them.

**Give to them courage in danger,
alertness of mind**

→

**and warmth of heart
that they may be guided
    to right decisions for the good of all.**

For clergy, ministers and pastors, and all who attend to our spiritual needs and bring to us the saving news, the encouragement, the guidance and the consolation of Christ – Lord, hear our prayer:
Lord, bless them and help them. Amen.

29.53   ABOUT TERRORISM
Editors

God of peace, we have been shocked by the sheer brutality and callousness of terrorist attacks. We have been numbed by the loss of life, saddened by the hatred of the fanatical, distressed by the power of destruction let loose upon innocent people.

Lord forgive us for any complacency:
Lord, forgive us.

Lord teach us how to love one another:
Lord teach us.

Lord pity us in our weakness:
Lord, pity us.

Lord enlighten us, and show all who are disaffected and embittered that the only remedy for grievance is the justice of the God of love and peace:
Lord enlighten us.

**Help us to put our faith in you,
and to work as peacemakers
in a distressed world.
We ask this for your glory. Amen.**

29.55   IN TIMES OF TROUBLE
From Psalm 143†

O Lord,
hear our prayer as we cry for your mercy;
in your faithfulness and righteousness
come to help us.

Do not bring us to judgement,
for no-one is innocent before you.

We remember days gone by,
and think about all you have done for us:
answer us now, O Lord,
and do not hide yourself from us;
for we put our trust in you.

We pray to you:
show us the way we should go,
rescue us from our enemies,
teach us to do your will,
and by your good Spirit
lead us in a safe path,
for your name's sake. **Amen.**

29.56   IN TIMES OF TROUBLE
From 2 Chronicles 20†

O Lord God of heaven,
you rule over states and nations;
power and might are in your hand,
and no-one can withstand you.
We stand in your presence
and cry out to you in the name of Jesus;
of ourselves we have no power
    to face an aggressor,
we do not know what to do –
but our eyes are on you. **Amen.**

29.61   FOR THE JUDICIARY
        AND POLICE
From 'A New Zealand Prayer Book'

God of truth and justice,
we ask you to help the men and women
who administer and police our laws;
grant them insight,
    courage and compassion,
protect them
    from corruption and arrogance
and grant that we,
    whom they seek to serve,
may give them the support and affection
    they need;
so may our people be strengthened
    more and more
in respect and concern for one another.
Amen.

29.62 FOR PEACE
Eric Milner-White, adapted David Silk

O God,
you desire to enfold
  both heaven and earth
in a single peace;
Let the design of your great love
lighten upon the waste of our angers
  and sorrows;
and give peace to your church,
peace among nations,
peace in our homes,
and peace in our hearts;
through Jesus Christ our Lord. **Amen.**

29.63 THANKSGIVING
         (REMEMBRANCE)
Editors

Our gracious and eternal God, we give
you thanks for the world you have
created:

We praise you for your great goodness to
your people in sending Jesus Christ to be
the Saviour of those who trust in him. O
Lord, we worship you:
from our hearts
  we praise and thank you.

Today especially, we thank you for all
who courageously served our country in
time of war. O Lord, we worship you:
from our hearts
  we praise and thank you.

We praise you for the graces of strength
and endurance given to our people in
these dark days of danger and sorrow. O
Lord, we worship you:
from our hearts
  we praise and thank you.

We give thanks for all who laid down
their lives for our sake:
make us worthy of their sacrifice,
help us to strive for peace,
make us loyal to each other
and above all to you, our God;
through Jesus Christ our Lord. Amen.

29.64 THANKSGIVING
From 1 Chronicles 29†

Lord God of our fathers,
may you be praised for ever and ever!

You are great and powerful, glorious,
splendid and majestic: Lord God of our
fathers,
may you be praised for ever and ever!

Everything in heaven and earth is yours,
and you are king, supreme ruler over all:
Lord God of our fathers,
may you be praised for ever and ever!

All riches and wealth come from you;
you rule everything by your strength and
power: Lord God of our fathers,
may you be praised for ever and ever!

Now, our God,
we give you thanks,
and praise your glorious name;
through Jesus Christ our Lord. Amen.

29.65 DEDICATION
Editors

Lord God our Father, we pledge
ourselves to serve you and all
humankind; for the cause of peace, for
the relief of need and suffering, and to
the praise of your name:

By your Spirit,
Lord, guide us.

From your wisdom,
Lord, teach us.

With true courage,
Lord, bless us.

In eternal hope,
Lord, keep us. Amen.

29.66 ACCLAMATION
From Isaiah 23 and 24†

Lord almighty,
you bring low the pride of all glory
and humble those who are renowned
  in the earth,
you stretch out your hand over the sea
and make the nations tremble.

→

To you we raise our voices
and shout for joy,
we acclaim your majesty,
we give you praise,
we exalt your name;
from the ends of earth we sing,
'Glory to the righteous One!'
for you will reign among us
for ever and ever. **Amen.**

29.67 DOXOLOGY
From Revelation 15†

Glory be to you, O God,
Father, Son, and Holy Spirit –
you have power, wisdom and majesty:
receive from us
honour, glory, worship and blessing.

Great and marvellous are your works,
just and true are your ways:
blessing and honour and glory
   and power
be to him who reigns upon the throne,
and to the Lamb,
through the one eternal Spirit,
now and for ever. **Amen.**

29.68 DOXOLOGY
From Romans 11†

O Lord our God,
how profound are the riches
of your wisdom and knowledge;
how unsearchable your judgements,
and your paths beyond tracing out!

**Who has known your mind, O Lord;
who has been your counsellor?
Who has ever given to you,
that you should repay?**

For from you and through you and to you
are all things:
yours be the glory for ever! Amen.

Acknowledgements

The Editors are grateful to all authors, publishers and other copyright–holders who have given permission for their works to be reproduced in this book. In many cases the attribution has been short enough to be included with the prayer. Where a longer credit was required full details are printed here.

Prayers by Frank Colquhoun are from the *Contemporary Parish Prayers* and are reproduced by permission of the author.
Prayers by William Barclay are reproduced by permission of SCM Press.

Prayers by Michael Hollings and Etta Gullick are from *The One who Listens* and are reproduced by permission of McCrimmon, Great Wakering, Essex.
The prayer by George Appleton from *One Man's Prayers* is reproduced by permission of SPCK.

Prayers from *Everyday Prayers*, *Further Everyday Prayers* and *When you pray with 7's to 10's* edited by Hazel Snashall are reproduced by permission of the National Christian Education Council

The Prayer by Zinnia Bryan is from the *Prayers for Children* and is reproduced by permission of Scripture Union.

Prayers from *The Promise of his Glory: Services and prayers for the season from All Saints to Candlemas* are copyright © The Central Board of Finance 1990, 1991 and are reproduced by permission.

Prayers drawn from the *Alternative Service Book* 1980 (ASB) are © The Central Board of Finance of the Church of England 1980, and may not be reproduced without permission. Inclusive language variations are those proposed by the Liturgical Commission of the General Synod of the Church of England in the paper GS 859 *Making Women Visible* which has only the authority of the Commission by which it was prepared. The variations have no legal standing at the present time but, in an answer to a Question in General Synod, the then president (Archbishop Robert Runcie) expressed the view that such amendments might be made in local circumstances.

Prayers from the *Contemporary Prayers for Public Worship,* and *More Contemporary Prayers* edited by Caryl Micklem are reproduced by permission of SCM Press.

Prayers by Elizabeth Goudge are from *A Diary of Prayer* and are reproduced by permission of David Higham Associates Ltd.

Prayers from *Worship Now* are reproduced by permission of St Andrews Press.

Prayers by David Silk are from *Prayers for use in the Alternative Services* and are reproduced by permission of Mowbray, a division of Cassell plc.

Prayers by Joyce Huggett are from *Approaching Christmas* and are reproduced by permission of Lion Publishing plc.

The prayer attributed to Edinburgh House Press is from *Daily Prayer and Praise* and are reproduced by permission of Lutterworth Press.

The song by Janet Lunt is reproduced by permission of Mustard Seed Music, PO Box 356, Leighton Buzzard LU7 8WP.

Scripture quotations taken from the *Holy Bible, New International Version* are copyright © 1973, 1978, 1984 by the International Bible Society, and are used by permission.

Scripture quotations taken from the *Good News Bible (Today's English Version), British usage edition* published by the Bible Societies and Collins, are copyright © American Bible Society 1966, 1971, 1976 and are used with permission.

The Jubilate Liturgical Psalms, also available in *The Dramatised Bible* published by HarperCollins, *Psalms for Today* and *Songs from the Psalms* published by Hodder & Stoughton, are copyright © 1986, 1989, 1992, Michael Perry/Jubilate Hymns; © 1986, 1989, 1992 Hope Publishing Company.

Readings from *The Dramatised Bible* published by HarperCollins and the Bible Society are copyright © 1986, 1989 Michael Perry/Jubilate Hymns; © 1986, 1989 Hope Publishing Company.

Prayers prayers and responses marked '✝' are from *Bible Praying* published by HarperCollins and are copyright © 1992 Michael Perry/Jubilate Hymns.

For assistence in preparing the manuscripts of *Prayers for the People,* people's edition and ministers edition: Rev Jane Austin, Bunty Grundy, Emma Hewlett, Isabel Izatt and Valerie Parker.

A Short Service

INVITATION
From Psalm 98†

Sing to the Lord, all the world,
for the Lord is a mighty God.

Sing a new song to the Lord,
for he has done marvellous things.

Proclaim his glory among the nations,
and shout for joy to the Lord our king.

GREETING
From Romans 1 etc.†

Grace and peace to you from God our
Father and from the Lord Jesus Christ.
Amen

APPROACH
From Psalm 118†

Lord,
this is the day you made;
we rejoice and are glad in it:
help us and bless us
as we come into your presence -
we praise you and exalt you,
we celebrate and thank you;
for you are our God
and your love endures for ever. **Amen.**

CONFESSION
From Psalm 51†

**Lord God, be gracious to us
because of your great love for us;
in your great mercy
wash away our sins -
for we are weighed down by them,
and we know we have failed;
we have offended against you
and done evil in your sight:
create in us a pure heart,
put a loyal spirit in us,
and give us again the joy
    that comes from your salvation. Amen.**

ABSOLUTION
From Psalm 103†

The love of God for those who seek him
is as great as the heavens are high above
the earth: as far as the east is from the
west he removes *your* sins from *you,* and
he will remember them no more. **Amen.**

EXHORTATION
From Revelation 19†

Let us rejoice and be glad,
and give God the glory. Amen.

BEFORE READING
From 2 Samuel 22†

You are our lamp, O Lord;
you turn our darkness into light.

AFTER READING
From Mark 4†

Those who have a mind to hear,
let them hear!

CREED
From 1 Corinthians 8 and 12†

We believe in one God and Father;
from him all things come.

We believe in one Lord Jesus Christ;
through him we come to God.

We believe in one Holy Spirit;
in him we are baptised into one body.

**We believe and trust in one God,
Father, Son and Holy Spirit. Amen.**

THE LORD'S PRAYER
From Matthew 6 and Luke 11

**Our Father in heaven,
hallowed be your name,
your kingdom come,
your will be done,
on earth as in heaven.
Give us today our daily bread.
Forgive us our sins
as we forgive those who sin against us.
Lead us not into temptation
but deliver us from evil.**

**For the kingdom, the power,
and the glory are yours,
now and for ever. Amen.**

BEFORE PRAYER
From Hebrews 4†

Let us approach God's throne with
confidence:
**we shall receive mercy,
and find grace to help us. Amen.**

FOR OTHERS: IN TROUBLE
From Psalm 31†

Be merciful, Lord,
to all those in trouble:
those who are ill or weary,
those who are deep in sorrow,
those whose life is ebbing away,
those who are without friends,
those who are forgotten by the world:
Lord, we entrust them to your care;
in Jesus' name. **Amen.**

FOR OURSELVES
From Isaiah 33†

Lord, be gracious to us,
for we long for you:
be our strength every day,
our salvation in time of trouble,
our greatest treasure in life,
and our reward in heaven;
through Jesus our redeemer. **Amen.**

THANKSGIVING
From Isaiah 63†

Our God,
we thank you for all your kindness,
and we praise you
for all the good things
    you have done for us:
you are our saviour -
in our distress
you too were distressed,
in your love and mercy you redeemed us;
through Jesus Christ our Lord. **Amen.**

THE GRACE
From 1 Corinthians 13

The grace of our Lord Jesus Christ,
and the love of God,
and the fellowship of the Holy Spirit,
be with us all evermore. **Amen.**

DOXOLOGY
From Romans 16†

Glory to God
who alone is all-wise;
through Jesus Christ, for ever! **Amen.**

BLESSING
From Numbers 6†

The Lord bless *you* and keep *you*, the
Lord make his face to shine upon *you*, the
Lord be kind and gracious to *you*, the
Lord look upon *you* with favour, and give
you peace. **Amen.**

A Communion Service

INVITATION
From Psalm 96†

Sing to the Lord a new song:
proclaim his salvation each day.

Declare his glory to all:
he is great and worthy of praise. Amen.

GREETING
From Ruth 2†

The Lord be with you:
the Lord bless you.

APPROACH
From Psalm 26†

Lord God,
we are here to worship you -
let your love guide us,
and your faithfulness lead us;
we come to ask for your forgiveness,
to gather round your table,
to bring you our thanksgiving,
and to proclaim your redemption:
receive the praise of your people. **Amen.**

COMMANDMENTS
From Mark 12†

Jesus said: Love the Lord your God with
all your heart and with all your soul and
with all your mind and with all your
strength; and love your neighbour as
yourself.
Lord,
we have broken your commandments:
forgive us, and help us to obey. Amen.

CONFESSION
From 1 John 1†

God our Father,
you have taught us
that if we say we have no sin
we deceive ourselves
and the truth is not in us:
we humbly confess our sins to you,
and we ask you to keep your promise
to forgive us our sins
and to cleanse us
**   from all unrighteousness;**
through Jesus Christ our Lord. Amen.

ABSOLUTION
From Psalm 6†

The Lord God be merciful to *you* and heal
you; the Lord turn his face towards *you*
and deliver *you*; the Lord save *you* in his
unfailing love; through Jesus Christ.
Amen.

EXHORTATION
From Psalm 107†

Let us give thanks to the Lord:
his mercy lasts for ever.

He satisfies the thirsty:
and fills the hungry with good things.
Amen.

BEFORE READING
From Jeremiah 9†

Let us listen to the Lord,
let us pay attention to his word.

AFTER READING
From Revelation 1-7†

Hear what the Spirit is saying to the
churches:
thanks be to God. Amen.

CREED
From Titus 2 and 3†

Let us confess our faith in one God, whose grace has dawned upon the world.

**We believe in God the Father,
who has revealed his loving kindness
to us,
and in his mercy saved us -
not for any good deed of our own,
but because he is merciful.**

**We believe in God the Son,
who sacrificed himself for us
to free us from our sin,
and make us his own people,
holy, and eager to do good.**

**We believe in one Holy Spirit,
whom God poured out on us
generously
through Christ our saviour;
so that justified by his grace
we might become heirs of eternal life.
Amen.**

INTERCESSION
From Hebrews 4 etc.†

Let us approach God's throne with confidence:
**we shall receive mercy,
and find grace to help
in time of need. Amen.**

Upon . . . have mercy, Lord;
we entrust them to your care.

In . . . Lord, may peace and justice rule:
let your love prevail.

To God be glory in the Church and in Christ Jesus:
for ever and ever. Amen.

PEACE
From 1 Peter 5†

Peace to you all in Christ: greet one another in love. **Amen.**

ACCLAMATION
From 1 Chronicles 29†

Yours, Lord is the greatness,
the power and the glory,
the splendour and the majesty;
everything comes from you,
and of your own do we give you. **Amen.**

GREETING
From 2 Timothy 4†

The Lord be with your spirit:
grace and peace be with you.

THANKSGIVING
*From Ephesians 5, Isaiah 6, Romans 5,
John 6, 1 Corinthians 11, and Psalm 19†*

In the name of our Lord Jesus Christ we give thanks for everything to God the Father. Father, we thank you for all your goodness, especially for . . .

Lord, high and exalted, yet present among us, with angels and saints in heaven we call to each other:
**Holy, holy, holy,
the Lord almighty is holy,
his glory fills the world. Amen.**

Pour out your love into our hearts by the Holy Spirit whom you have given to your people. Let this bread and wine be to us the body and blood of Christ, food of our eternal life.

For our Lord Jesus Christ
in the night he was betrayed,
took bread,
and when he had given thanks,
he broke it and said,
'This is my body, which is for you;
do this to remember me'.

In the same way, after supper,
he took the cup, saying,
'This cup is the new covenant
in my blood;
do this, whenever you drink it,
to remember me.

$\rightarrow$

So may our remembrance
be acceptable in your sight,
O Lord our strength and our redeemer.
Amen.

THE LORD'S PRAYER
From Matthew 6 and Luke 11

Our Father in heaven,
**hallowed be your name,
your kingdom come,
your will be done,
on earth as in heaven.
Give us today our daily bread.
Forgive us our sins
as we forgive
    those who sin against us.
Lead us not into temptation
but deliver us from evil.**

**For the kingdom, the power,
    and the glory are yours,
now and for ever. Amen.**

BREAD AND WINE
From John 6†

Jesus said, 'If you come to me you will
never go hungry.' **Amen.**

Jesus said, 'If you believe in me you will
never be thirsty.' **Amen.**

DOXOLOGY
From Romans 16†

Glory to God
who alone is all-wise;
through Jesus Christ, for ever! **Amen.**

BLESSING
From 2 Thessalonians 3†

The Lord of peace give *you* peace
at all times and in every way;
and the blessing of God almighty,
the Father, the Son and the Holy Spirit,
be with you always. **Amen.**

DISMISSAL (MORNING)
From John 20†

Jesus said, 'As the Father has sent me, so
I am sending you.' Go in the name of
Christ. **Amen.**

DISMISSAL (EVENING)
From Exodus 33†

The presence of the Lord go with you:
the Lord give us rest. Amen.

The resources for Holy Communion within this volume have been devised to meet a need in
some free churches. In the Church of England, elements may commend themselves for use where
the rubrics or canons allow.